WE NEED TO TALK ABOUT
THE FUNERAL

This book is dedicated to:

Percy Morrell
1909 - 1962

Peggy Worlock (Morrell)
1913 - 1989

Susie Smith
1955 - 1997

Robert Nutbeem
1954 - 2000

WE NEED TO TALK ABOUT THE FUNERAL

101 ways to commemorate and
celebrate a life

Jane Morrell & Simon Smith

alphabet
& image
PUBLISHERS

Alphabet and Image Publishers
77 High Street
Totnes
Devon TQ9 5PB

Published by Alphabet and Image Publishers 2006

ISBN 1-899296-31-X
ISBN 978-1-899296-31-6

A CIP catalogue record for this book is available from the British Library.

The publishers and authors disclaim any injury, damage, loss or liability connected with the use of the activities in this book. There may be unintentional errors or omissions. In this case, please contact the publishers.

Printed and bound in China by Compass Press on paper supplied from a managed resource.

Contents

where and when to hold the funeral 54

burial and cremation 65

the funeral ceremony 78

resources and information   178

Front cover image by Rosie Sanders. The authors would like to thank all the photographers for permission to reproduce their images, especially those who generously opened up their portfolios.

acknowledgements

green fuse was launched with a brave vision in 2000 and is indebted to Ruth Jenni, Rachel Laine, Rebecca Barnstaple for their pioneering spirits, Don Thornford, Phil Thornford for their extraordinary talents with flowers and photography.

For sharing the vision, John Fox and Sue Gill of Welfare State International, Mike Jarvis of the Natural Death Centre, Dr Tony Walter of Reading University, James Roose-Evans of Bleddfa, Prof. Malcolm Johnson of Bristol University, Rupert Callender, Mahesi Caplan Faust, Carol Aston, Paula Rainey Crofts, Hazel Selina.

For support, encouragement, and harsh and exciting comments throughout the project, Wild Geese.

For giving us feedback on the drafts of the book, Jim Jervis, Sophie Banks, Dr Jonathan Shaw, Georgina Tisdall, Annie Mitchell, Ruth Binney.

For vision and encouragement, Miranda Spicer our publisher, and our design and production team, Susan and Andrew Sutterby, and all who have helped and advised us over the last six years, we appreciate you.

Special thanks to Annabel Milln, John Haggar, Debbie Carnegie, Hannah Nutbeem, John and Nikki Spurr, Claire Ballard, Rod Nelson, Jane and Jon Dunn, John Evans, Fred Christopher, Andrew Lithgow, Dr Linda Durman, Brian Perring.

foreword

From the moment you start reading this book you think, 'Why on earth didn't someone think of writing this years ago?' It genuinely satisfies a long felt want because we are far too squeamish to discuss or even think about our own deaths.

The Victorians were much wiser. They knew the good of thinking about death well in advance and took interest in every detail. They saved money to pay for their funerals, sometimes finding it hard to afford it, but feeling a sense of security when they had actually done so. This splendid book will offer you all the options and all the possibilities you might want to think about, give you a guide on costs and, above all, will make life much easier for your family and friends. What could be a better legacy for them than that?

Claire Rayner

introduction

What do you do when someone dies? How do you arrange a funeral? You may have more idea about what you don't like about funerals than what it is you would like and we have brought together 101 practical points to give you information and to help you make choices.

The funeral rites and ceremonies of your religion are part of worship and may offer you great comfort, but if you do not attend a place of worship on a regular basis, like four out of five people in the UK, you may be looking for a more individual approach to funerals. All the ideas in this book have come from our work with clients over the last six years, to give you enough information to take charge to the extent that feels right along with the necessary reassurance to help you fulfil your wishes.

There is no expectation to hold a 'perfect funeral', but rather an appropriate, heartfelt one. Families, friends and communities can move away from convention to reclaim choice over how to hold a funeral and experience how important this is for grieving and remembrance.

As part of our work as funeral conductors we hold discussions and talks about death, funeral arrangements and ceremonies. We meet people who have a desire to talk candidly about death and what funeral directors do. We have heard a powerful voice demanding more participation by the bereaved in caring for the body and in the funeral ceremony, to bring in more heart and soul to complement the already efficient procedures. It is refreshing to see more women becoming involved with funerals in the roles of clergy, funeral directors and conductors.

Our main objective is to give a perspective on funeral arrangements that is rarely heard, enabling you to find your own way to think about and achieve what you want. We suggest a starting place to think about how to choose poetry and music specifically for the person who has died and we recommend existing anthologies. We do not examine the funeral rites of specific faiths, but offer ideas and perspectives, which might appeal to anyone looking for a funeral that does not adhere strictly to a tradition. Our intention is not to create a rival to traditional religious practices but to be inclusive of tradition and innovation. A personal, open-hearted and memorable funeral serves the spiritual beliefs of the person who has died – and the bereaved.

Our experience has shown that small gestures can improve a funeral and make it more personal and heartfelt, which is why some simple ideas, which can transform the whole experience, are included. Alternatively, you will find here what you need to create a wildly unconventional funeral if you wish.

We appreciate enormously the courage of all the individuals and families who have engaged in the challenging process to find the right place, music and words in order to create a heartfelt ceremony at times of overwhelming grief. Their persistence to give their loved ones the best possible funerals and ceremonies they could has been an inspiration to us personally and professionally, and provided the basis for this book, which we hope will inspire more people to do the same. We particularly thank those who agreed to share their stories and photographs as a way of passing on their experiences.

This book is designed and organised into sections and numbered points so you can easily access the information you want. It is a book to dip into and therefore it has been necessary to repeat some information in different sections, for clarity.

Jane Morrell & Simon Smith

getting organised

Being organised enough and making clear decisions are difficult when you are bereaved. Giving yourself time to make the best decisions you can will help you. Even when a death occurs with some warning most of us are surprised by the sense of shock and ensuing turmoil of complex emotions.

When someone dies it is natural to rush into taking decisions. It is very difficult, perhaps impossible, to make all the right choices at such an emotional time. The most valuable first thing you can do is to ask someone to help and support you, and to take up genuine offers of assistance. If there is not such a person, and even if there is – we hope this book will be a support for you at a difficult time.

This section covers arranging a funeral for someone immediately after their death. The ideas will give you the time and resources to:
• work out what you want without feeling pressurised
• stay as much in control of the process as you can
• get what you want without overspending your budget
• look after yourself during the period between death and the funeral
• create the funeral you want

Families' wants and needs are very diverse. Some want to do as much of the arranging and looking after the person who has died as they can, and others prefer to seek as much help as possible from funeral directors. It can be really difficult to know what you would like to do if you do not know what is involved. This book is based on choices: what you can do if you want to – and only if you want to and feel able to. Take a deep breath and pause. When a life draws to a close it is worth taking a little extra time. You do not need to rush into decisions and tie up all loose ends straightaway.

1 ask for and accept help

Before you make any decisions ask someone to come and help you if at all possible – to be your ally, comforter and sounding board. Ask a friend or relative, preferably someone who will be a calming and stable influence and, ideally, who has arranged a funeral before. If you have been a carer for some time and managed on your own, you may not be used to approaching others for help or taking it when it is offered. But often on these occasions it comes from both likely and unlikely places.

In many cultures the bereaved family are looked after by friends and the community, who bring cooked food and help with shopping, cleaning, chores and arrangements. If others are willing to do these practical things for you it gives you more time to make the arrangements you want to make and start to come to terms with your loss. You need time to sleep and rest, as the emotional upheaval is always exhausting.

> To help another human being cope with a death is a privilege. We all need the opportunity to face death from time to time and remove the hold it has over us, to make it more familiar and take away its strangeness. To know death is to know freedom. Whoever has learned to die has learned to live.
>
> *Simon Smith*

2 take time to make decisions

Following a death, promise yourself a decision-free twenty-four hours to talk things over with your family, friends and anyone helping you to arrange the funeral. Take time to make informed decisions and do not be afraid to ask questions. People who love you may try to protect you from painful choices and situations, but do what you feel you need to do. Taking time allows you to look for and think about any views the person who has died might have had about their death and funeral.

If the person died naturally at home or from a terminal illness and a doctor has seen them during the last fourteen days, and you are sure you do not have to involve the emergency services, it can be comforting to sit with the person for a while to say goodbye to them quietly. When you are ready, the district, community or Macmillan nurse will help you, so that the person who has died can remain in your care at home if you wish. Only fifty years ago it was commonplace for people to die and be cared for at home, but now eight out of ten die in institutions and are cared for by the funeral director.

If you prefer, call a funeral director and explain that you want them to collect and look after the body until you have made more decisions. Ask them how much it will cost just to do this. It is still possible to change to the funeral director of your choice once you have thought things through.

If the person died in hospital they will be held in the mortuary and usually can remain there for a day or two until you decide what you want to do, depending on how busy the mortuary is. If someone dies in a care home or hospice they will be taken to the duty funeral director's premises, but you can still switch to your chosen firm of funeral directors later.

3 gather quotes from funeral directors

'Once someone approaches a funeral director, on almost all occasions some sort of funeral is usually sold. 92% of people visit just one funeral director' according to the Office of Fair Trading's 2001 report on the funeral industry.

In our work as funeral advisers we gather quotes for clients from two or three different funeral directors to ensure value for money. For example, we recently obtained three quotes from funeral directors to assist with a woodland burial of £975, £750 and £520 for exactly the same work. This is not unusual in our experience. Coffins purchased directly from the funeral directors, especially cardboard, woven and unusual ones, vary greatly in price.

Most of us have little idea what funeral directors will do or charge for specific services. This is an awkward time to negotiate. It is easy to think that the more you spend the greater the respect you are showing. To ask someone less involved to obtain three cost estimates enables you to put any embarrassment aside and spend more of your budget on the things you want. You can copy the template on page 188 and use it for obtaining quotes from funeral directors. Cross out the things you do not want and ask them to fill it in and return it to you.

Your right to know

Funeral directors must fully itemise their estimated charges as part of their industry code of conduct. Beware funeral directors who try to sell you a package, quoting for example '£1,300 plus disbursements'. You are within your rights to choose exactly the parts of their services you want and to know how much each part will cost you. If they will not give you this detailed information, we suggest you do not use them.

4 **six important questions**

If you can answer the following important questions, you will feel more able to proceed with confidence and peace of mind. Reading through this book will help you to answer them.

1. Are you aware of any written or spoken preferences of the person who has died concerning their funeral arrangements?
2. Do you need to choose between a burial and a cremation?
3. If burial, have you chosen a cemetery, local parish churchyard, woodland or natural burial site? Have you considered a burial on private land?
4. Would you like to look after the person at home for some or all of the period before the funeral?
5. Do you already have a preference for a funeral director, or do you need to choose one based on research?
6. Would you, your family and friends like to have some active involvement in:
- caring for the body
- decorating or making the coffin
- the content of the funeral ceremony
- conducting or participating in the ceremony?

5 when and where to hold the funeral

B's mother, when she was dying, insisted that B and her husband J take the two-week holiday they had booked. She died two days before they were due to go. They arranged for her to be cremated during the first week of their absence and held a funeral ceremony with her ashes present a few days after they returned.

Unless you are to follow family or religious tradition, or are constrained by a coroner's inquest, choose the date and time for the funeral that suits you best. Up to two weeks after the death is usually fine. It is best not to leave it too long because life often feels like it is 'on hold' until the funeral has taken place.

You may need to contact many people in order to decide. You can wait a few days until you have found the best day and time before you need to book a place for the ceremony, crematorium, or burial place.

Around one in five deaths is referred to a coroner, but very few go further than a brief preliminary investigation.

6 who should come?

Funerals are usually open to everyone who knew the person. They are informed about the funeral rather than invited. There may be times when the close family feel the need for a private ceremony. In these circumstances a public memorial service is often held at a later date.

You may have a dilemma about children attending, struggling with whether or not to 'put them through' the funeral in the hope of protecting them from a harsh reality. It is usually better to include the children and try to find gentle ways of telling them about death which they will find possible to understand, either before or as part of the funeral.

There is a wonderful book by Doris Stickney called *Water Bugs and Dragonflies* which explains death to young children and which could be read to them. Another good book for older children is *What On Earth Do You Do When Someone Dies?* by Trevor Romain, which could be read and talked about during the time between the death and the funeral. See page 194 for bereavement services.

The day I didn't go to the funeral – Jane's story

It was a week before my tenth birthday, a clear sunny April day, when my father came home early from work and went to bed. This was highly unusual, unknown even, and sensing my anxiety mum bid me not to disturb him. Half an hour later, unable to contain my desire to see him, I tiptoed in. The curtains were drawn, the room shadowy and in tiny breaths I asked him how he was. He asked for a drink of lime juice and although we had no way of knowing, it was the last contact we ever had. A few hours after his death that afternoon my mother gathered my brothers and myself and told us that we were not to talk about him, he had gone and she couldn't bear any reminders. The week was spent in hushed tones behind closed curtains and nobody explained anything to me. Someone at some point said, sorry, but the best time for the cremation (what was that?) would be on the following Friday, my birthday.

Big black cars parked in the drive and as my family were climbing in someone told me that I would be dropped off at a friend's to play for the day. I was dumbfounded. The car stopped further up the road and I bolted into my friend's back garden heading for the safety of our den at the top of the rockery, and there I stayed, on my own, for the entire day. I sat quiet and still in the shrubs watching the circulating water fall down the rocks and was turned over by a tidal wave of emotions I had never experienced before: confused, lonely, angry and abandoned. Suddenly, somehow, I didn't belong with the family (had I done something bad?), I wasn't good enough to go with them, and I felt like an outcast.

In the following weeks no one spoke about him, no one asked me how I was feeling, and within four months I was away at school with a completely different set of rules to figure out. Thirty years later a tidal wave of grief hit me.

A child's chance to say a proper goodbye – Hannah's story

When I was twelve my father died. It came as a big shock; luckily my mum and step-dad were really supportive and caring. They encouraged me to take an active role in the funeral. Mum came up with the idea of a drape, to go over the coffin whilst in the church, and to be buried with him. I designed it and doing so gave me a sense of purpose for the funeral.

I decided to incorporate the things that he loved and things that reminded me of him on the drape. Mum helped me draw a hand planting an acorn and out of the wrist of the hand was an oak tree. Around the edge of the drape I painted Native American symbols for things that he loved. We also scanned some photos of important people in his life and stuck these on the oak tree.

I chose a song that reminded me of him to be played at the funeral.

Seeing the drape and hearing the song was a moving experience. It helped me feel some sort of connection to his death.

It was definitely a positive experience to be involved in the funeral. I am very glad that I took the time to create something that connected me to him and say my last goodbye.

I would say it is good to involve children as much as possible in a funeral as it could help them come to terms with the death of a loved one and give a sense of purpose in those last precious moments.

7 how to choose a funeral director

Your relationship with the firm of funeral directors is vital. Their role is to help you to arrange the funeral of *your* choice. At first, many people feel like Michele, 'I knew what I did not want, but did not really have any idea about how to get what we did want.'

Decide as far as you can, what it is you want the funeral director to do and the desired level of involvement of family and friends in looking after the body and designing and conducting the funeral ceremony. Quality of service is also important and far more difficult to judge in advance of using the services. Recommendations from other people are helpful, but find out what sort of funeral they arranged. A good funeral director for a traditional funeral in a church may not be the right one if the family want to actively participate in the arrangements. For example, you may want an alternative venue or to use a woodland burial site, or even keep the body at home for a vigil the night before the funeral ceremony. Gauge how helpful, flexible and open to your ideas the funeral directors are. Their attitude to your cost survey will provide you with information, for example whether they are prepared to quote for exactly what you want rather than give you a price for a package.

If you and others are likely to want to view the body, see if they have a pleasant and spacious chapel of rest in which you could spend some time, and make sure their visiting hours are sufficiently flexible.

Remember that if the person who has died is with the duty funeral director or if they died at home and you telephoned a funeral director in a panic, you can still change the choice you have made. It is important to make a positive choice. There is no need to feel uneasy about this. Such a decision is within your rights, details of which are published in the National Association of Funeral Directors' code of conduct.

Increasingly funeral directors are owned by big corporations, but still trade largely under the old family name. Ask a funeral director whether they are an independent family firm or part of a group (the biggest groups are Co-operative Funeralcare and Dignity).

The website of the Association of Independent Funeral Advisers, www.funeraladvisers.org.uk, will clarify if there is a funeral adviser in your area who could help you to choose an appropriate funeral director. Alternatively, The Natural Death Centre has a national list of recommended funeral directors and can be telephoned on 020 7359 8391.

8 family-led funerals

The information in this book will help you choose the level of involvement you and your family would like and be clear about the services you want the funeral director to supply. We have found there is an increasing demand for information, choice and participation. You will find information on registering a death, forms and paperwork on pages 180–186.

A few well-resourced and well-informed families choose to make most or all of the funeral arrangements, carry them out themselves and require very little assistance. In *Funerals And How To Improve Them*, Dr Tony Walters says: 'Funerals are seen as too expensive because they do not work. They are impersonal because they have been bought and not lovingly put together by the family or the community.' Greater involvement does tend to make the funeral a more personal event. If things the family have put together do not go entirely to plan, the mistake is usually seen sympathetically, perhaps comically. But when the professionals make a mistake, the reaction often includes anger and disappointment.

For further information on dying, death and family-led funerals see *The Natural Death Handbook* (recommended further reading, page 196). Or see if there is a funeral adviser in your area by calling the Association of Independent Funeral Advisers on 01803 840 779 (www.funeraladvisers.org.uk) or approach an independent funeral director for advice.

Saying goodbye to Mum – Annabel's story

How one woman took her mother's funeral into her own hands

During my mother's final illness, I broached the subject of doing her funeral myself. We had talked openly about death and she was fully accepting and prepared for it. You might ask, 'Why go to the trouble of doing my mother's funeral, when there is a whole industry devoted to the disposal of bodies?'

I decided that I wanted to take back what had been lost and conduct her funeral from start to finish. It turned out to be a most empowering experience. The process of preparing her body, decorating the coffin and conducting her funeral service was an honouring of her life and a true gift to her in death.

I was with her when she died at 5.15a.m. and stayed with her for the next three hours. The hospital staff were very supportive. It gave me the chance to begin to come to terms with the reality of her death.

Laying out her body with the assistance of the nurse was a uniquely special and sacred moment. Handling her lifeless body continued the process of making her death more real. We washed her, put in place an incontinence pad and dressed her in a white Victorian nightie that she had chosen as her shroud. I then asked for more time alone with her: time to remember, meditate and grieve.

The porter wrapped her in the required plastic shroud and I accompanied him to the mortuary. While I was there, I checked the access for loading the coffin into the car. I took the hospital paperwork to the registrar at the local District Council offices, who issued a death certificate.

Next, I went to the nearest crematorium with the death certificates and forms and booked the funeral for a week's time. I paid the crematorium invoice before the funeral. They agreed that a cardboard coffin was acceptable.

The coffin was delivered to my home and I started the process of decoration. Selecting photographs from hundreds to make a montage for the lid of her coffin helped me look at her life again and our times together, both sad and joyful. It helped me to really see this woman from youth to old age and to grieve her loss and the passing of her life. The montage was an honouring of her life and making the coffin as beautiful as I could was a gift to her. I painted the coffin gold and glued beautiful paper to the lid.

My two brothers, and sister (who had agreed to my 'DIY' funeral) could not

come over for the funeral from Australia, so I asked them for contributions to the ceremony. One brother requested 'September Song', which he remembered Mum and her best friend singing over and over again to a gramophone record when he was a child. My other brother and my sister asked me to say things on their behalf. I wrote a poem about my mum and myself, which moved me deeply.

On the day of the funeral, a friend and I drove to the hospital in an estate car, which was long enough for the coffin. I had been dreading the moment because I had no idea what to expect. I was a bit shocked at how Mum's body had become shrunken because of the cold and the death process – it definitely brought home the finality of her death. Having a friend there was a tremendous support.

I took a photograph of Mum's body with a rose on her chest for my brothers and sister, to help them grieve. Then we closed the coffin, put it in the car with quite a struggle, as there were only three of us, including the porter, to carry it.

We drove to the crematorium where we met the other mourners. The cremation staff were very helpful in carrying the coffin from the car onto a trolley and into the chapel. Meanwhile, I explained how I wanted to run the ceremony, which was very simple and personal. I interspersed talking about Mum with music, messages from my siblings and close friends, my poems and the psalm. People said how moved they felt. A friend took photographs throughout the ceremony.

Overall, the whole experience of dealing with my mother's death was a deeply moving and wonderfully creative one. It was so simple and ordinary, yet sacred and was an experience I would not have missed, which will stay with me for the rest of my life.

9 decide how much to spend

How much you spend depends on what you want, where you live and how much you can afford. As you can see from these examples, at 2006 prices, you have a choice of how to spend your money. When deciding your budget, there are three important factors to take into account:

1. What you can realistically afford, or how much the person has set aside in a pre-payment plan.
2. The type of funeral which seems most appropriate e.g. you might not arrange a lavishly expensive funeral for a thrifty person.
3. A realistic assessment of what funerals cost.

As a guideline £1,000 will buy a simple funeral, or one in which the family is very involved, possibly with a burial on private land or a local churchyard. Most funerals fall in the £1,500 to £3,000 range and you can spend more.

By looking at these examples and getting quotes from funeral directors, you should be able to put together an accurate budget for what you want.

Some examples of funeral costs:

Every funeral director should offer a Basic Funeral, which normally includes:

• initial interview for arrangements
• utility transport
• two bearers only (they use a trolley)
• a plain chipboard coffin without handles

Basic funeral with burial in churchyard

Basic funeral package	*£700*
Churchyard burial with service in church and verger	*£160*
Total	**£860**

Cremation with full funeral director involvement

Funeral director's fee for	
transport and care of body, hearse, limousine and bearers	*£950*
Bamboo coffin	*£350*
Cremation fee	*£400*
Doctors' certificates	*£124*
Clergy	*£105*
Urn	*£ 50*
Notices in newspapers	*£100*
Flowers	*£300*
Total	**£2,379**

Burial with family involvement to care for deceased and provide bearers

Funeral director's fee for arrangements	*£400*
Transport and some care of body, hearse	*£200*
Willow coffin	*£650*
Burial plot and interment fee	*£800*
Funeral conductor's fee and help to design ceremony	*£150*
Hire and decoration of village hall	*£200*
Food and drink	*£200*
Release of homing pigeon	*£100*
Total	**£2,700**

Burial on private land largely arranged by family

Funeral director's fee	
to collect, look after and release the deceased	£150
Cardboard coffin (bought direct)	£100
Grave digging	£200
Funeral adviser's fee	£150
Funeral conductor's fee	£150
Hire and decoration of yurt	£400
Food and drink	£300
Flowers	£200
Musicians	£150
Total	***£1,800***

how to pay for it

A funeral can be paid for out of the estate if there are sufficient funds. Often the executor will instruct the bank to release money for the funeral before probate has been settled. This is easier if the request is for one or two payments clearly related to the funeral and the bank makes the final decision.

Whoever arranges the funeral also takes on the responsibility to pay for it. As the arranger, if you do not have sufficient funds to pay for the funeral or you are not willing to finance it, you may be able to raise a loan from the deceased person's own bank, repayable by the estate.

The Department of Work and Pensions will pay the cost of burial or cremation and up to £700 of other costs for a basic funeral where the estate of the person who has died and family members have no savings and the next of kin is claiming benefits.

10 a 'telephone tree'

Depending on the circumstances, perhaps the age or situation of the person who has died, there may be many people to contact about the death and funeral, or if only a few, they may be difficult to trace.

Make a list of people you would really like to talk to personally and ask someone to help you inform others. Having tried to tell everyone about the death and funeral of my partner, I spent many hours a day on the telephone, repeating the same things and trying to help others through the shock. Although there were some people I wanted to talk to, I found this totally exhausting and emotionally draining.

Ask your helper to make a list of as many people as they can find to inform about the funeral, from address books, Christmas card lists, e-mail addresses, latest e-mails, mobile phone numbers and business files.

By organising everyone into categories, for example close and distant family, work, clubs, old school friends, current friends, etc., one prominent member of each group can be responsible for calling others, so that everyone is included in a 'telephone tree' and informed in good time for the funeral.

A notice in the local paper will reach a lot of people and an announcement in their favourite national paper or their trade or hobby magazine might be appropriate.

It is worth asking someone, either the funeral director, conductor, or a friend to organise a method of collecting the names of everyone who comes to the funeral, for example by giving each person a blank postcard to fill in.

planning in advance

It is immensely beneficial to do some planning for a funeral beforehand. It gives more time for difficult choices to be thought about and discussed at a time when there is less pressure. This section is for those who feel able to plan or start planning their own or someone else's funeral in advance of the death.

Death is not much talked about, but some who are dying would like to talk about their funeral. It gives them a reason to think and talk about the end of their life, their life story and their wishes and it can relieve a sense of isolation. Talking about the funeral can be a way into a painful subject. Often, to have spoken about the inevitable, opens up an intimacy which can make the whole process of death somehow less frightening. Marie de Hennezel's *Intimate Death*, is an extraordinary book which tells us how to talk to the dying and how to deal with death.

A was dying of cancer. He was under the care of a hospice and looked after at home by a Macmillan nurse, in whom he confided. He was anxious to talk to someone about his funeral and to tell his story in his own way. I visited him at his home and sat with him for a couple of hours listening and taking notes. Later the nurse called me to say A seemed so much happier and more settled since talking to someone. The information about his life formed the basis of the eulogy.

To make plans for your own funeral takes some strain and anxiety away from your family. To help someone prepare theirs is a rare privilege. If you are arranging a funeral, it feels better and more organised not to have to guess what the person would have chosen. Many people struggle with quite fundamental and stressful questions, such as whether to opt for burial or cremation. You may find it is easier to do this when you are feeling healthy and robust.

11 **write down your funeral wishes**

Browsing through this book will help you to think about ideas for your own funeral, or if you want to discuss a funeral with someone who is dying.

A funeral marks the end of a life and is primarily about the person who has died, but it is for the living as well, so beware tying everything up so tightly that those left behind cannot contribute. D was a gardener with no partner or children, but many friends. When he died he left strict instructions: there was to be no funeral at all and he was not to be mourned. Everyone felt devastated. Instead they held a memorial service for him in his special place out in the woods and scattered his ashes among his favourite snowdrops.

Other close relatives and friends may want to contribute, so either discuss it with them at the time you are writing the plan, or leave enough gaps and opportunities for them to have a say too. They are not obliged to follow your wishes.

When you have written down your wishes, make sure the document can be found. If you have a funeral guardian, give them a copy and let your next of kin know to contact this person in the event of your death. If your solicitor is the only one to have a copy lodged with your will it may be discovered too late. So let your executor, partner, spouse, relative, friend or even all of these have a copy.

An idea which works well for a local group of women is a get-together once a year over a few glasses of wine. They review their funeral plans – everything from readings and music to types of coffins or urns – and make changes if they want to, in this informal atmosphere. They say the subject matter always seems to provoke much humour and laughter.

12 planning payment

It can be heartbreaking for a family when they cannot afford
the funeral they want, or the funeral the deceased has
requested. It can be a great help if you put the money aside,
between £1,500 and £3,000, depending on your requirements
and location. Given the recent upward trend of funeral costs,
it is worth reviewing the amount from time to time and
topping it up if necessary. There are three widely used options
for making sure the money is available:
1. A high-interest bank or building society account.
2. A life insurance policy which will pay out the desired amount.
3. A prepaid funeral plan.
It is worth talking to an independent financial adviser before
proceeding.

**Depositing the money into a high-interest bank or building
society account** is the simplest way to ensure it is available at
the time it is needed, with the greatest flexibility. Open a joint
account with your executor or next of kin which allows
immediate access, so they can withdraw the money when it is
needed for the funeral. When someone dies their sole-name
bank accounts will usually be frozen, so a specific joint account
avoids the funeral arranger having to finance the funeral and
claim the money back when the estate is settled and the
funds released.

Life insurance can be taken out to pay a lump sum on death which would cover the funeral costs. Premiums vary depending on your age and health. It is more difficult to adjust this kind of arrangement to take account of price rises.

A pre-paid funeral plan, usually sold by a funeral director, is a scheme whereby you pay for your funeral in advance in a lump sum or in instalments. These plans guarantee you a funeral at today's price, except that many of them have a clause that allows the provider to charge an excess for above-inflation rises in costs outside the direct control of the funeral director (for example fees for cremation, doctor's certificates and burial).

The main disadvantage of these plans is that many are based on standard packages and can be inflexible if you or your family want to amend your plans or change your choice of funeral director, so it is worth reading the small print. Most have a cancellation charge.

The advantage these plans provide is peace of mind. Not only has your funeral been paid for, but also the basic arrangements have been made.

We recommend that you only purchase a pre-paid funeral plan that states that your payments are invested in a reputable trust fund, and which is affiliated to the National Association for Pre-paid Funeral Plans or the Funeral Planning Council or is approved by the Financial Services Authority.

13 officially appoint your next of kin

You can nominate anyone to be your next of kin, a member of your family, spouse, co-habiting partner or friend. Your next of kin would be informed in the event of an accident or your death, given information about your medical condition, consulted about your treatment in hospital (they can represent your views but not make medical decisions), and be first in line to make your funeral arrangements unless you have appointed a separate funeral guardian. A next of kin has no legal liabilities, rights to your medical notes or to your personal possessions and assets. Nominating your next of kin does not affect who would inherit from you either.

You could carry a next of kin card (make your own, or download one from www.advicenow.org.uk) with the name and details of your choice. You should discuss it with whoever you choose to nominate, and perhaps close relatives you have chosen not to nominate. Also let your other friends and family know who you have nominated to ensure they are informed.

14 a funeral guardian

When L died her funeral was arranged by her relatives, whom she had not seen for many years and with whom she had never been very open about her life and beliefs. Her many friends felt inconsolable after her funeral, because the traditional Anglican ceremony just did not reflect her views of life at all. As one said 'it just wasn't her'.

Appointing a funeral guardian can ensure this situation is avoided. Their role is to lead the planning and organising, while remaining sensitive to the needs of the closely bereaved and ensuring that their, and any of the wishes of the person who has died, are carried out as far as possible. One vital early role is to work out a brief for the funeral director and to obtain quotes for the work.

A funeral guardian has no legal status if there is a dispute. They may be a friend, your next of kin or a relation or someone you know who is willing to find out about arranging a funeral and to give the time when it is needed.

A funeral guardian

- is able to devote time for planning and, hopefully, to give several days of his or her time in the week after a death
- is far enough removed from the situation to remain calm and organised
- will listen to you, understand how you want the funeral to be, and speak up for you
- is organised and assertive

15 be a funeral friend

Once you have found out about funerals and thought about your own, you could provide a useful service to your friends, relations and social and community groups by offering to be a 'funeral friend'. Should any of them need to arrange a funeral you could be on-hand to give them guidance and support.

If you are interested in being a funeral friend, you might be interested in joining the Funeral Friends Forum. Their website is www.funeraladvisers.org.uk. You will receive a regular newsletter of up-to-date information and ideas to help you serve others.

caring for the body

C's mother died at home. C decided she did not want her mother's body to be disturbed for twenty-four hours. She helped the nurse make the body secure and comfortable, and left her lying peacefully on her bed in a cool room. Friends and relatives came to visit and sit with her body. As this arrangement worked well, C kept deferring the funeral director's visit to collect her mother. In the end, she kept her at home for three days, surrounded by those who loved her. Many felt that this had helped C's mother to make the transition from this life to the next, and they gained great comfort and a sense of completion from spending time with her body.

You may feel that you would like to participate in caring for the body of the person who has died during the time leading up to the funeral. You have choices as to how they are looked after. Until relatively recently, it was commonplace to bring them home, as is still the case in many countries and religious traditions. Now that the dead are so neatly and quickly tidied away, many people have become unfamiliar with them and fear them.

Some who spend time with the body, tending and caring for them, praying for them and sitting with them, find their view of death is profoundly changed as they gain a sense of the life or soul leaving, perhaps to continue its journey. Being faced with an empty shell that once held the life of the person, in its stillness and final peace, can be a profoundly moving experience, particularly if the person had suffered pain or injury before dying. Fear of the body dissipates and an understanding of what it is to die, grows.

16 spend quiet time with someone who has just died

'I can't believe how lovely it was just to sit with Mum, quietly, for a few hours after her death.' K

You may also find spending some quiet time with the person who has died a lovely experience. Talking to them may help you come to terms with their death. Saying the things you feel you need to say, whether they be expressions of love or hurt, anger or disappointment, disbelief or feelings of abandonment, can be freeing. In the long term, this may help you to move towards acceptance of your loss. Other very close family and friends may also be grateful for this opportunity to visit someone they love in familiar surroundings. It can also be an intensely religious experience for people of strong faith.

> When I die I want your hands on my eyes:
> I want the light and wheat of your beloved hands
> to pass their freshness over me once more:
> I want to feel the softness that changed my destiny.
>
> Pablo Neruda, extract from 'Love Sonnet LXXXIX'

The restless tides have stopped. I sit with you, looking for tiny signs of life; there are none. You have gone. I sit with you, quiet, tender, still, our last time together before the world comes crashing in. You look so peaceful, complete, like this is where your life was supposed to end. I steal this time with you - a last hour - to say goodbye, and thank you and good luck. I would not miss this moment for the world. I too feel strangely at peace, complete, a sense that all is well. Like a calm before the storm, the grief can now come. You live on in my memory, forever.

Simon Smith

17 **laying out**

Traditionally the women of the household or community would wash and lay out the dead. In many parts of the world, particularly in 'the West', this tender task has gradually been taken over by nurses and, in some cases, funeral directors. But it is a caring and often comforting activity in which to participate if you feel you want to.

If you would like to do this, unless you have done it before or have help from someone who has, ask the district, community or Macmillan nurse to assist you. It takes two people. If you are in a hospital or care home, you may ask to be involved.

There are times when this may be a much more challenging task in which you may not want to participate, for example if the body has suffered injury, infection or surgical intervention. If in doubt, seek advice from the nurse.

The act of laying out is to make the body comfortable, clean, dry and secure. For more information see page 187.

18 anointing with oils

Anointing a body by massaging oils into the skin is an ancient rite and, if you feel you can, is lovely to do, giving a real sense of looking after the person to the very end. It helps to keep the skin supple. Set aside about a cup of basic massage oil (grapeseed or sweet almond) infused with ten drops of essential oil, for example myrrh or frankincense, which have a preservative effect. Rub small amounts of this mixture into the skin. If you prefer you may find simply rubbing oil into the hands or face a pleasant experience. The earthy, mossy, woody, spicy essences tend to be more sympathetic than the sweet smelling, flowery ones.

The Ancient Greeks used to favour oil infused with marjoram (*Origanum vulgaris*), which has preservative and cleansing properties. The Greeks believed that marjoram growing on your grave was a sure sign the spirit was at peace. Frankincense is said to help the spirit make the transition from this world to the next, and leave the past behind. The picture is a photomicrograph of myrrh.

19 **favourite clothing**

J was upset to see her father lying in his coffin in what she could only describe as a woman's nightie. It was, in fact, a mortuary gown, something he definitely would not have wanted to be seen dead in!

People often used to be buried in their 'Sunday Best'. If you wish, you can dress the person in their favourite clothes. Increasingly clothes and shoes are made with man-made fibres which will not be acceptable to natural burial sites or crematoria, so if you are choosing clothes, they should be made from natural materials like wool, cotton and linen. You will need someone to help you. Rigor mortis will set in six hours after death, but will gradually wear off after twenty-four hours, so it is easiest soon after death, or a day later. Always be very gentle when moving or turning a body. If you do not want to dress the body yourself, ask your funeral director to do it.

Jewellery and objects made from metal, glass and plastic are not allowed by crematoria and must not be put in the coffin. There is a real danger of explosion and injury to attendants. Emissions are strictly monitored for each cremation.

20 caring for the body at home

If you want to do this make sure you follow the guidelines below. The body does not need to be held in a mortuary for the whole time between the death and the funeral. In most circumstances you can look after the body at home, if you want to and if you feel you can, for at least some of the time, unless the body is needed by the coroner or the person had a highly contagious disease or infection. The guidelines for keeping a body at home for up to a few days are:

1. If you are unsure about looking after a body, get advice from the nurse who has attended, or from the district nurse. If neither is available, contact another medical professional or a funeral director, particularly if the person underwent treatment with drugs such as chemotherapy, surgery or suffered physical injury before death.
2. Wash and lay out the body to make it comfortable, clean and secure. Clean and dress any wounds. Lay the body on absorbent material or an incontinence pad. Put a pillow under the head.
3. Use the coolest room in the house, preferably north facing, turn off any heaters and draw the curtains to keep out direct sunlight.
4. Ventilate the room well and use fans to allow air to circulate.
5. If the weather is warm, hire a portable air-conditioning unit to cool the room. Wrap ice packs or dry ice in towels and place them under the back, on the torso and around any wounds, making sure they do not touch the skin as they will discolour it. Keep a second set in the freezer and change as necessary.
6. Burn incense, keep flowers and herbs in the room or use air fresheners.
7. The body does not have to be in a coffin. It can remain on the bed.
8. You can keep the body at home, without viewing, kept covered with heavy cotton material and with the lid on the coffin.

21 **visiting the body**

You may wish for the friends and relatives to have the opportunity to visit the body of the person who has died to say their last goodbyes. It is usually at the chapel of rest of the funeral director, but can be at home. The chapels of rest are often fairly grim, and as you usually have to make an appointment, visit within working hours and feel time-constrained, home often feels better.

When someone has died their skin takes on a pale and waxy appearance. Funeral directors often recommend embalming the body and perhaps restoring the looks of the person who has died. Embalming is rarely necessary. It has a preservative, and possibly hygienic effect, and may be done if there is more than two weeks between death and the funeral, or if the person underwent treatment with strong drugs, for example chemotherapy, or suffered physical injury before death. It is a good idea to avoid embalming, as it is an unnecessary expense and an unpleasant process: many green burial grounds will not accept embalmed bodies because of the toxicity of the chemicals.

We do not tend to restore looks cosmetically in the UK, generally accepting the person as they were at the end of their life. If you want to, or feel it is necessary to cosmetically adjust the look of the person before they are visited, make sure that whoever is going to do it has a photo to work from, so that they do it accurately. Visitors can find that it is upsetting when the deceased does not look as they did in life. As an alternative, you may simply want to apply a little make-up yourself, if that is what the person wore in life.

We know one funeral director who has made a beautiful and relaxing space for viewing, who provides comfortable chairs, tea, biscuits and ample time. This is an invaluable service for those wanting to see the person who has died for the last time.

22 **transport to and from home**

Transporting the body yourself from the mortuary to home or to the funeral parlour is legal, as long as the body is kept completely covered at all times. If you want to do this, and have the means, it is a good idea to have a coffin ready, or to wrap the person in a shroud, large heavy blanket or body bag and strap them onto a stretcher.

Only a few domestic vehicles are large enough to accommodate a coffin, so make sure you measure accurately before you start. Keep the body as flat as possible. You might want to warn your immediate neighbours when you are going to do this.

You can make arrangements with the mortuary yourself, or ask the hospital bereavement officer to liaise on your behalf. Let them know when you will be arriving and what help you might need. You need to take the death certificate with you. When you fetch the person from the mortuary there should be a trolley, which will make it easier for you to slide the coffin into the back of your vehicle. Mortuary staff are not obliged to help you, but often will. When you arrive home, you will need at least four, and possibly six, people to lift. Before you lift a coffin by the handles, make sure they are weight bearing, because some are only for show.

23 **holding a vigil**

When P died in his early twenties, the whole town was shocked. Unusually, his parents were offered a beautiful room in a natural health centre in which to let his body lie. Over the next few days a vigil was held, with someone always there. Many people of all ages and particularly his peer group came to spend time with his body and each other, to chat, play music, tell stories about him, laugh and cry. Each day they held prayers and meditations. This vigil was an important part of his family's, friends' and the town's coming to terms with his death.

The ritual of keeping a vigil for the recently departed is as ancient as mankind, but often overlooked in our daily rush to keep life ticking along as normal. A vigil could be held at your local church or place of worship or at home, for a few hours or a few days, immediately after death or just before the funeral ceremony. Simply inviting family and friends to sit with the body to mourn, reminisce, pay their last respects and take comfort from each other in a friendly and welcoming environment, where you will not be interrupted or rushed, can create a heartwarming and straightforward ritual where memories and emotions are shared.

You could have some time for readings, silence, prayers and meditation as well as time for talk. It is lovely to create an atmosphere by lighting candles and incense sticks, and perhaps having some soothing or inspiring background music. We recommend a plentiful supply of tea and biscuits. Some vigils are more formal, depending on your spiritual or family traditions, and led by the head of the family or a minister.

Some religions and traditions believe the soul leaves the body gradually, perhaps within a day or, for example in the Tibetan Buddhist tradition, over three days. For this reason many wish to leave the person as undisturbed as possible and to hold a vigil to keep watch over them and pray for the soul's safe departure.

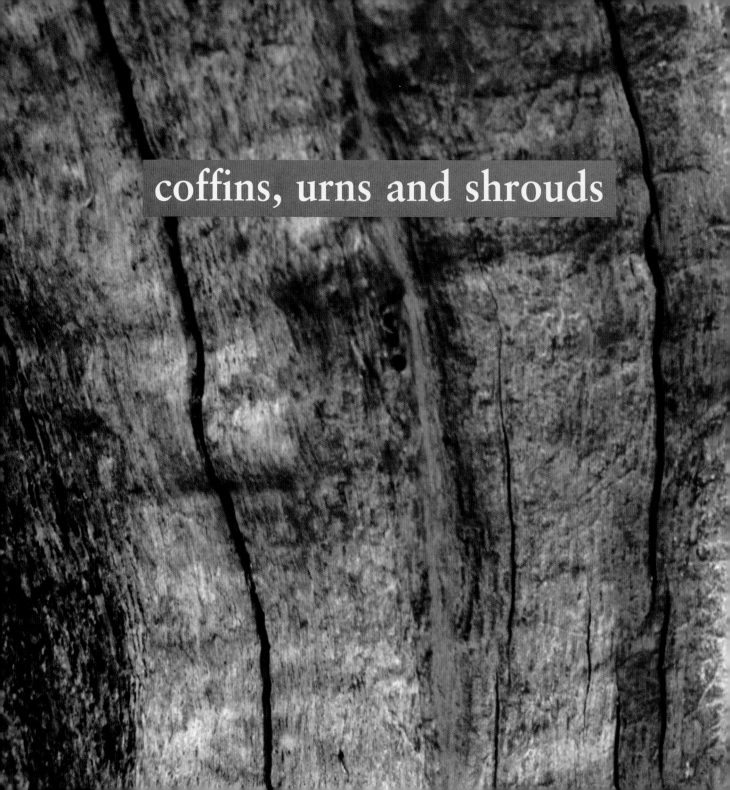

coffins, urns and shrouds

Coffins have been used for the famous and wealthy for a very long time, perhaps lined with lead to keep the elements out, but until the mid-nineteenth century most people would have been buried in a blanket or shroud. The Victorians, with the rise of the funeral director and a wealthier, more status-conscious population, made the coffin an innovation and from that time the vast majority of people have been buried or cremated in coffins.

Shrouds are now rarely used, but will appeal to the environmentally conscious as a natural and beautiful alternative. In England, from 1685 until 1814, everyone had to be buried in a woollen shroud, a measure to protect the wool trade. Failure to comply led to a hefty fine of five pounds.

Urns are used for the temporary or permanent storage of ashes. The urn, or just the ashes, may be kept, buried, scattered or thrown into the sea.

24 **the range of coffins**

Never has there been such an array of different types of coffins as there is now: wood, veneered chipboard, bamboo, willow, cardboard and papier mâché, and other variations such as laminated, pod shaped, American casket (lid opens in two halves), Italian 'Last Supper'. You can hire a reusable outer coffin for cremation. They may be decorated with motifs and colour, novelty varieties, rapidly biodegradable and more; it is quite a dizzying array. Some even have built-in sprung mattresses!

You have time to make a choice, so do not feel pressurised. A coffin is generally not needed until the day before the funeral and most are delivered within forty-eight hours, some within twenty-four.

If you want to choose a particular coffin for yourself or you want to have it ready for decoration, you could buy one in advance and store it. Some people use them as sewing, blanket or storage boxes. Although this might seem a little odd or unusual, the fact that it is around can make death seem more ordinary.

On what criteria do you make a choice?

• the choice of coffin reflects the personality of the person who has died
• it suits the type of funeral you are planning
• you like the look of it

- the price fits your budget
- the crematorium or burial site will accept it. Many crematoria now accept cardboard, bamboo and wicker coffins – check with them first
- environmental factors (e.g. made from sustainable resources, without chemicals and fully biodegradable)

Illustrated here are coffins you may not have seen before, all of which can be purchased direct from the manufacturer or through a funeral director. Full contact details are on page 192.

1. Bamboo Eco Coffin made by SAWD Partnership. They make other designs, children's coffins and also willow coffins.
2. Earthsleeper papier mâché coffin made by Andrew Vaccari Ltd. You have a choice of five colours.
3. Flatpack untreated pine coffin made by Eco-coffins. Easy to assemble. Good for painting. Made from FSC sustainable timber.
4. Pictorial cardboard coffin made by Greenfield Coffins. There are many to choose from or you can send them a digital picture for the design. They also make a range of coloured designs e.g. marbled effect, and plain ones ideal for painting.

5. Willow Coffin made by Somerset Willow Company also make round-ended and children's coffins. The picture shows one being made; see also page 121.
6. Ecopod papier mâché coffin made by Arka. These come in a range of colours and designs.

Coffins were once made by the local carpenter and there is no reason why you should not make or commission a handmade coffin, perhaps using wood from a wind-blown tree or reclaimed pine. Make sure it is not too heavy.

Ordering a coffin

Size: you need to know the height, weight and shoulder width of the person who has died.

Remember to order a lining, which can be made of cotton or a thin (preferably biodegradable) plastic.

Say if you need weight-bearing or decorative handles.

If you will be viewing the person in the coffin, order a 'pillow'.

Check the delivery time.

You can organise the purchase through a funeral director and some will sell you a coffin even if they are not providing you with any other services.

Some coffins can be purchased direct from the manufacturers at retail prices. It is easier to source the specialist ones this way than conventional veneered chipboard or wood.

25 decorating a coffin

A coffin can be painted, or pasted with pictures, posters and designs. If you, your family and friends are comfortable to gather together to share this activity it becomes a time to tell stories, laugh and cry together. As designs are discussed and decided upon, and materials gathered, memories will surface and can be shared. Decorating the coffin is an activity in which children can become involved and it can encourage them to ask questions about death and to talk about how they are feeling.

You may feel that you would like to take the time to decorate a coffin on your own. This is a very intense and personal task and you will have the space to think deeply and reflect on many memories.

Cardboard, smooth chipboard or MDF coffins are best for home decoration. In order to have enough time to decorate the coffin before the funeral, you should ideally have it delivered prior to death. If you feel confident about your artistic abilities, you can sketch out your designs and begin. If you feel less confident, you could paint it a favourite colour, onto which you could stencil motifs. An artist could sketch your ideas onto the coffin and you could fill in the colour, or ask them to do so. Pictures of different kinds can make an effective montage. If you want a uniform pattern, use high-quality wrapping paper or wall paper.

Materials

If there is to be a cremation or natural burial use only water-based paints, pastes, glues and natural, biodegradable materials such as cotton, hemp or linen.

Oil-based paints, solvent-based glues, metals and synthetic fibres are banned from crematoria and natural burial sites.

26 **a drape for the coffin**

A coffin drape designed for the individual is like a story book, reflecting the person's life and interests. It can be humorous, touching, happy, sad, surprising, informative and beautiful, bringing comfort and interest to family and friends who can add their own mementos. It is not about artistic merit.

For R's funeral the family made a coffin drape using a heavy piece of cotton onto which they painted motifs, wrote words and glued photos. At the funeral, this encouraged everyone to go and stand around the coffin. The drape was buried with R, once it was photographed, as a memento to be kept afterwards (see picture, left, and Hannah's story on page 11).

To make a drape, use a piece of material, plain linen, light canvas, hemp or untreated cotton, and cut it to drape generously over the coffin, at least 3 m x 2 m (10 ft x 6 ft). After the service the drape can either remain with the coffin on its journey, or be displayed and then taken home as a keepsake. The process of making a drape is similar to that of decorating a coffin (page 48); it involves the gathering of people and materials, if it is to accompany the coffin for cremation or a natural burial and decisions have to be taken on the design. Inspired by patchwork quilting traditions, one family found a local seamstress to make a colourful and lively drape from clothes and embroidered material.

Decorating a drape is a good alternative to painting a coffin, especially if it is difficult to have a coffin delivered to your home or if you feel it will be too distressing to encounter the actual coffin. It can be easier for children to be involved in preparing a drape. Take time over it, as the process of making it can be comforting and therapeutic, and it is about honouring the person you are remembering. If it does that, everyone will love it.

27 **a beautiful urn**

Urns contain ashes which can be stored before scattering or more permanently, interred for burial. Most commonly plastic, ceramic or metal, they are available in many materials, including biodegradable clay, papier mâché, cardboard, bamboo and willow. There is even one made of compressed salt and sand and another of gelatine and sand, which will sink to the bottom of the sea or river and dissolve within a few hours.

Any container with a wide, tight-fitting opening at the top or base and volume of at least 2L will do, for example, Chinese ginger jars and beautiful wooden boxes. Alternatively you could buy a plain one and decorate it yourself, as you would a coffin. If you just want to keep a small portion of the ashes you could put them in a locket with a strong clasp. For details of suppliers, see page 192.

1. Raku fired ceramic urn from Artefacto Ceramics. They make a range of designs, including biodegradable clay urns.
2. Bamboo urn from SAWD Partnership. They make other designs too.
3. Neptune sea urn made by Regale Memorials from compressed sand and salt, slowly dissolves in water.
4. Papier mâché acorn urn made by Arka.

28 make or buy a shroud

Shrouds have been used since ancient times and make a beautifully simple and environmentally friendly alternative to a coffin. Traditionally made of wool they may also be made of cotton, linen, hemp or felt. Unfortunately it is difficult to buy them nowadays because so few are used, but, it is quite easy to make your own.

A young woman who was dying was in a great state of agitation. Her friend knew she was terrified of being closed in a box and told her that she would be wrapped in a soft woollen shroud. Her anxiety diminished and she died peacefully.

The picture shows a handmade felt cocoon shroud made by Yuli Somme of Cocoon Designs. A contemporary design taken from an ancient practice, this felt shroud offers an alternative to a coffin, made from Devon wool and 100% natural materials. Contact details can be found on page 192.

To make a shroud you will need:
- a piece of natural material measuring at least 3 m x 2 m (10 ft x 6 ft). It need not be hemmed or finished but cut it with pinking scissors to prevent fraying
- two pieces of cotton padding, 2 m x 1 m (6 ft x 3 ft) or thick blankets
- a piece of strong wooden board the length and shoulder width of the body e.g. 180 cm x 60 cm (6 ft x 2 ft)
- three pieces of strong rope, each 3 m (10 ft) in length, possibly black

To make a shroud:
1. Place the three ropes parallel and horizontal on the ground, 0.5 m (18 in) apart.
2. Place the shroud material with the long edges vertical over the ropes with the centre rope at the centre of the shroud.
3. Secure each rope to the material at the central point by stitching it or stitching on a loop of material to pass it through.
4. Place the board in the centre of the material so it is evenly placed over the three ropes, cover it with cotton padding or blankets and place the body on that.
5. You can put cotton padding over the body to give it a smooth outline.
6. Fold the material over from one side, and fold the ends in.
7. Fold the material over from the other side and fold the ends in. The body should now be entirely covered. You may want to put a few stitches into the folds to hold it securely in place.
8. The ropes are the means of carrying and lowering the body into the grave.

You could provide your funeral director with the materials and ask them to make it up for you. To purchase a shroud kit, contact green fuse on 01803 840779 or www.greenfuse.co.uk. To buy just the fabric, log on to www.loopfabric.co.uk.

where and when
to hold the funeral

Most funerals are currently held in places of religious worship and at the ceremony halls of cemeteries and crematoria. Religious buildings are evocative spaces, each one individual, often ancient, with beautiful carvings and decoration, a place that has seen much of life, joy and sadness. Entering one of these buildings is in itself a ritual act, moving out of the hustle and bustle of the normal world into a hallowed and sacred place. It is no surprise that they remain popular even with those who do not regularly attend them.

The ceremony halls at crematoria are used only for funerals, although a few of the newer ones are being designed to accommodate other ceremonies; they are non-denominational. The architecture and interior design of most ceremony halls is often vaguely like twentieth-century churches, but, sadly, blander than a plain biscuit, because they need to be suitable for use by people of different faiths, individual spiritual beliefs or no faith at all. Many complaints are made about their impersonal, sterile, almost industrial feel, yet so many funerals take place in them.

As people have become more secular, or spiritual without formal religion, more choice of locations is needed, akin to the demand for wedding locations. There are no legal restrictions on where a funeral can be held (with permission of the owner of the site) and no licences are needed, so the choice is even wider than for weddings.

This section describes the wide range of choices available, and what you should take into account when choosing the place and time for the funeral ceremony.

29 possible venues

You can hold a funeral ceremony with the coffin present anywhere that will agree to have it. There is no licence needed. If you do not wish the ceremony to be held in a religious place of worship or a crematorium, you could try

- a village or local hall
- a function room in a hotel or pub
- a boat usually hired for parties
- the register office (purely secular ceremonies only)

A funeral can also be held

- at home
- in the garden

or if you want the funeral and the burial to take place together

- at the graveside
- at a woodland burial ground
- on your own land or on other private land

A funeral can be held in any of these places prior to cremation. You may have more ideas of possible venues in your area.

If you have a favourite church that is not your local one, it is worth asking if you can hold the funeral there.

When choosing a place you need to consider:

The permission of the owner: you must have this and do not be surprised if you are refused, death is an emotive subject.

Privacy – you do not want members of the public to walk in on the funeral inadvertently.

If in a public building being used for other things at the time, ideally the room will have its own separate entrance to the outside.

Good access to carry a coffin in and out, so look out for narrow entrances, tight corners and stairs.

Adequate parking.

Sufficient seating.

Easy access for the elderly and disabled.

Availability of toilets and refreshments on the premises or nearby.

30 **avoid the 'conveyor belt' funeral**

Just because there is to be a cremation does not mean the funeral ceremony has to take place at the crematorium. There are more complaints about the time limits and the 'conveyor belt' feeling of being sandwiched between the last and next funerals than any other aspect of funerals.

The main funeral ceremony can be held before the cremation and then as few or as many family and friends as desired may accompany the coffin to the crematorium just for the committal.

The cremation could take place first, followed by the main ceremony with just the ashes present. If you do this you should be aware that part of the objective of a funeral, with the committal of the body either to the earth or the fire, is to emphasise the reality of the death. If you only have the ashes present, or a memorial service without a coffin or ashes, it is even more important to represent the death symbolically in order to gain that final sense of completion. For example, a candle could be extinguished or a photograph or object signifying the person removed.

F was cremated with just a simple committal at the crematorium chapel for her very close family, before a funeral ceremony was held at home for her wider family and friends later that day. It would not have been possible to have the ceremony at home with the coffin present because of access and space.

31 more time at the crematorium

A twenty-minute service at the crematorium often seems too much of a rush, giving insufficient time to do justice to a whole life. Others feel it is enough at such a raw time. If you want more time, many crematoria will allow you or the funeral director to book a 'double slot', especially if outside the busiest hours of noon and three p.m. Some crematoria will not charge any more for this, some double the fee, but most charge an additional amount of between £40 and £80.

Taking more time gives you a few minutes to decorate the space simply, perhaps with a few objects, or your own flowers. It gives a few more minutes to gather and settle before the ceremony begins, and allows a longer ceremony.

32 marquees and yurts

P's funeral was held in her garden, a place that she loved. As it was winter and the house was not large enough to accommodate everyone, the family thought about hiring a marquee, but then came across a yurt, a large, round, white Mongolian tent which is wonderful for ceremonies (see pictures). With a diameter of 8.5 m (28 ft), it was large enough to accommodate about eighty people. The floor was strewn with richly coloured carpets and the yurt was heated by a woodburning stove, adding to the cosy, warm atmosphere, but at the same time the wind and the birdsong could be heard. Leaves that fell and stuck to the outside could be seen through the material, so it was self-decorating too!

There is a surprisingly large number of yurt hirers which you can search for on the web, or you may find some in the marquees and tents section of *Yellow Pages*.

33 an outdoor ceremony

Traditionally, many funeral ceremonies took place outside around the graveside, but this is now relatively rare. However, with the growing popularity of woodland burials this is becoming more common again.

There is something very special about funerals held outside, for example in a garden or a wood, or even nearly outside, as in a marquee or yurt. Being outside emphasises that death is a natural part of life, when we are enfolded back into the earth or scattered to the elements as ashes. Outside, you can see the views, hear birdsong and running water, feel the wind, which is symbolic of change and spirit, be aware of the fiery warmth of the sun and feel the earth, to which we return, beneath your feet. Outside, we become more aware of the world we leave when we die, with its joy and its sadness, the fallen leaves and the emerging buds and flowers. The only thing you do not want is too much water in the form of rain.

34 the best day and time

Unless required by the tradition of your faith, there is no particular rush to have a funeral. It is best to arrange it for the most convenient time for everyone. But be aware that you may feel like you are in state of limbo until the final resolution of the funeral.

Crematoria are very heavily booked, especially around Christmas and New Year, so a longer timescale may help you to get your favoured time of day.

35 weekend funerals

It is possible to hold a funeral and cremation or burial on a Saturday, even a Sunday, if you are not dependent on funeral staff. Traditionally, funerals are held on weekdays during working hours because of staffing. Generally, crematoria, cemeteries and funeral directors charge up to twice their normal fee on a Saturday, amounting to perhaps an additional £500, depending on your local prices. If it means everyone can come you may decide it is worth the extra expense.

We helped with a family-led funeral on a Sunday, followed by burial on their own land. Most of the family and friends, many of whom had a long way to travel, could come on that day and did not feel under time pressure.

burial and cremation

Making the choice between burial and cremation can be difficult. This section looks at burial and cremation and the widening options for burial in the new natural and woodland burial sites and on private land, as well as in cemeteries and churchyards. You can also be buried at sea, but only a handful of these take place each year and it is a difficult process, so we do not recommend this unless you are absolutely determined.

Many churchyards and cemeteries, especially in large towns and cities, are full or nearly full, and alternative forms of burial grounds are needed. You would be deemed quite fortunate to be able to be buried in your local churchyard, and cemeteries are now selling leases on graves as short as thirty years. Crematoria are very busy and many feel impersonal.

Whether choosing for yourself or for someone who died without stating a preference, your choice between burial and cremation may be intuitive, you just feel one is more acceptable or less frightening than the other, may be based on family or religious tradition or on environmental factors.

In Sweden, there is a new process being developed, where the body is broken down through freezing; it is buried close to the surface and soon becomes useful compost.

36 **deciding between burial and cremation**

If the person who has died did not leave express wishes, choosing between burial and cremation might be the most difficult decision you have to make. You may prefer the symbol of a body being returned to the earth and becoming part of it, or the symbol of a body going to the fire and its associations with purification.

You may also be strongly influenced by family traditions, with the family having been buried in a particular place for generations; or perhaps their ashes have been scattered or interred in a particular place over time. Where it is not possible to make another burial on an existing plot, it is quite common to have a cremation and then spread or inter the ashes there.

Once seen as the modern, streamlined, hygienic approach to disposal of the body, as advocated by the founders of the Cremation Society, the image of cremation has been overshadowed by concerns over environmental issues, dissatisfaction with the impersonal nature of the ceremony and surroundings, and a need to be more in touch with the processes of death and dying.

Whether you choose burial or cremation you do have a choice as to where you hold the funeral ceremony, and after cremation you will have another chance to commemorate with the ashes present. You can hold the funeral ceremony with the coffin present in all sorts of places, but eventually the body will need to go to either a crematorium or a burial site. Often a service in church is followed by a short committal at the crematorium. There are no hard and fast rules about who goes to the committal. It could be the entire congregation, just close family, or nobody. When you use an alternative site for the ceremony you may find that decision especially hard to make if you are a close relative. Not going to the crematorium can also leave you with a feeling of emptiness and non-completion.

37 **natural, green and woodland burials**

Natural burial and green burial are terms used for returning a body to the earth in the most environmentally friendly way possible. Natural burial grounds may be in nature reserves, flower meadows, woodlands or fields being turned into new woodlands or meadows. These burial plots are often in beautiful surroundings.

In 1995 Ken West, the bereavement officer for Carlisle, set up the first woodland burial site in the UK. The three main objectives were to:

• provide an alternative, more natural environment for the bereaved
• reduce ongoing management costs of burial grounds
• use the land to provide a wider range of environmental benefits

Through the process of organising these woodland funerals in Carlisle some families realised that they could create much more personal and satisfying funerals by participating in making the arrangements and organising the ceremonies themselves. These family-led woodland funerals are often referred to as 'green

funerals'. The initiative has proved extremely popular and now there are over two hundred natural burial sites across the UK and around five thousand burials each year, with new sites opening all the time.

Over the years the people who have come to us asking about 'green funerals' do not necessarily want a woodland or natural burial, rather they are asking for information about how they could participate more and do things differently. They do not want to repeat the dreary experience of their aunt's twenty minutes at the crematorium when the officiant even got her name wrong. They want to participate in the funeral arrangements themselves to make it more personal and more representative of the person they love and have lost.

Some of the woodland sites are owned and managed privately and some by local authorities. Many are small, a few acres, but some are much larger with planning permission for thousands of burials. Only a few have buildings on them in which funeral services can be held, but they are generally set up with good vehicular access.

Headstones are often not allowed in order to keep the integrity of the natural site. Often, instead of a headstone, a tree will be planted close to the grave. If headstones are allowed they are usually small and laid flat on the ground. Increasingly the grave is being marked with a microchip or GPS coordinates so that the graves can be identified. Once the site is full it is left to nature.

The sites are not usually consecrated and therefore are open to people of any or no religion. There is no reason why you should not have an individual plot blessed by a religious minister if you wish.

The cost of a plot is usually in the range of £500–£800 including the cost of digging the grave and interment.

To find a site near you contact the Association of Natural Burial Grounds at the Natural Death Centre at www.naturaldeath.org.uk or telephone 020 7359 8391. Clothes must be of natural fibres; materials for coffins, coffin liners and shrouds must be completely natural and biodegradable such as:

- plain untreated wood
- bamboo or willow
- papier mâché
- wool, hemp, linen or cotton shrouds

38 churchyard or town cemeteries

By the middle of the nineteenth century, many churchyards were full and burial plots were used time and time again. In 1832 private cemeteries (i.e. not belonging to the parish) became legal under an Act of Parliament. A ring of seven private ceremonies were established around London. The 'Magnificent Seven' appealed to the newly emerging middle class and their ornate gravestones were seen as a public extension to the family's property. These historically and socially important graveyards are now largely managed as wildlife havens.

Recently there has been growing concern about safety in cemeteries as a result of injuries and deaths caused by falling headstones. Tight controls over the supply and fixing of memorials are in place and increasingly only selected, approved masons are being allowed to work in cemeteries. Check that your supplier has accreditation to work in the cemetery of your choice and that the type of stone, its shape, size and inscription you wish to use, is permitted. To use a town cemetery contact the town clerk. The availability of space and cost of interment varies widely. For example the cost in Croydon is around £3,000 for a single plot, whereas the same in Monmouthshire would cost £240 (2006 prices).

Similarly the availability of space in a churchyard varies from parish to parish and you may not assume that you can automatically be buried in the parish where you were born if you no longer live there. It is worth enquiring to see if you can reserve a place. This decision is at the discretion of the local parish priest and the cost is consistent across the country.

The parish fees for funerals in 2006 are:

Service in church, cemetery or crematorium	*£87*
Burial in churchyard following on from service in church	*£160*
Burial in churchyard without church service	*£193*
Burial certificate, if required	*£12*

published by The Ministry Division, The Archbishop's Council of the Church of England,
Church House, Great Smith Street, London SW1P 3NS

39 **burial on private land**

P said she wanted to be 'planted' on her land when she died. Her family were delighted to find there is no law to prevent a burial taking place on private land, as long as the death has been registered and a Certificate for Burial issued (see page 184). They found that up to two non-commercial burials can be made on a piece of private land with the landowner's permission without a change in planning permission. They needed to adhere to the Environment Agency guidelines (see page 190) and they talked to the local environmental health officer to be on the safe side.

They decided on a plot of land with its own access, which they could put into a trust should they want to sell the remainder of the property in the future. Otherwise a new owner could possibly have the body exhumed and moved to a cemetery.

The family sent the tear-off portion of the Certificate for Burial to the registrar. They accepted the risk that the burial may affect the value of their property. As there was an acre of land, they thought this risk would be minimal, which may not be the case in an ordinary suburban garden. They had no mortgage on the property; otherwise they would have needed to notify any individual or mortgage company that has an interest in the property.

This form of burial allowed the family to organise a very personal funeral, over which they maintained total control. With costs significantly reduced by avoiding the cost of a burial plot and only minimal help from a funeral director, they could spend their budget on making the funeral exactly as they wanted. They talked to the neighbours to make sure they were happy with and understood the situation.

There is a statutory requirement for the landowner to maintain a register of burials, so they bought a notebook, especially for the purpose, wrote it in there and keep it somewhere safe and secure.

For more information on private land burial rules and recommendations, see page 190.

Carry me upon your friendly shoulders and
Walk slowly to the deserted field.
Take me not to the crowded burying ground lest my slumber
Be disrupted by the rattling of bones and skulls.
Carry me to my special field and dig my grave where violets
And poppies grow not in each other's shadow;

'The Beauty of Death' from Tears and Laughter
Kahlil Gibran

40 **cremation**

The Cremation Society was founded in the late-nineteenth century. Its main arguments, in favour of cremation, were based on burial wasting valuable land and cremation being more hygienic. From a slow and controversial start, cremation has increased in popularity since 1940, until now approximately seventy percent of bodies are cremated. There are over two hundred and forty crematoria in the UK, mostly owned by local authorities, but private companies are buying into the market and occasionally building new ones.

Crematoria ceremony halls are non-denominational and have no religious connotations. You may ask for any religious icons to be removed, or replace them with images from your own faith or religion. You can have the ceremony and funeral conductor of your choosing. Most halls have 'gardens of remembrance', where ashes can be scattered or interred.

The main complaint about crematoria is that they are busy. Their buildings are often uninspiring and add to the feeling of an industrialised place. People do not like to see the previous, and the next, mourners as they take their 'slot'.

Cremation avoids the use of precious land for burial. Being committed to the fire is final and unequivocal. Cremators burn a great deal of energy and release carbons and significant amounts of metals, such as mercury, into the atmosphere. Crematoria are bound by legislation, which requires increasingly expensive emission control, and this cost is passed on to the public. But, in many areas, cremation is still cheaper than burial, because of the high cost of plots.

41 do you receive the right ashes?

A common concern is whether, after cremation, you receive the right ashes. Crematoria have strict control and monitoring systems. The paperwork that must be filled in before the body is accepted is designed for efficient identification and confirmation of the cause of death. Each coffin must have a nameplate attached to it. This identification accompanies the process to the very end when the ashes are placed in a container ready to be collected. The cremated remains are comprised of bone material.

If you are interested to know how a crematorium operates you may ring up your local one and request a visit. Most are open to this.

42 **ecological burial**

A truly ecological method of burial has been designed by Susanne Wiigh-Mäsak from Sweden, based on her studies as a biologist and her knowledge of composting.

The body is frozen in liquid nitrogen, and then exposed to vibration when it disintegrates into dust. Metals including mercury are extracted and the remaining powder is placed in a coffin made from maize or potato starch. The coffin is buried in a shallow grave, which turns into compost in six to twelve months. A plant can be set on the grave. It will then grow, absorbing the nutrients released, as a symbol of the organic circle of life.

The process is called promession and Susanne's company is Promessa Organic AB.

At the moment there is no promator (the name given to the machinery) operating outside Sweden, but Promessa Foundation has applied for patents in thirty-six countries including the UK. For more information visit www.promessa.se.

the funeral ceremony

To clarify the process of organisation and decision-making this section on the ceremony itself has been broken down into four different parts:

• preparation for a ceremony with heart and soul
• decorating a beautiful ceremonial space
• the arrival of the coffin
• words, music and ritual

Today it is unusual for families and communities to have significant influence over the ceremonies connected with death. In the weeks following the funeral, many of us wonder why we feel incomplete; we are empty, angry and distressed with a feeling something has been missed out. If the brief ceremony has failed to connect us intimately to the person we knew, we may feel their whole life has been undervalued, put away in a few seconds in the words of a stranger who never knew them.

If you have never done anything like this, the process of organisation may feel difficult, but we have seen many 'different' ceremonies work well for so many people that we feel confident in urging you to take courage and follow your heart to create a ceremony full of meaning. With the right help and support, it is a wonderful thing to do. If you scan through the ideas in the following pages, allowing your attention to be caught by particular points, these ideas may be the ones to help you.

With so few people now attending a place of religious worship regularly, and four out of five people agreeing that secular funerals are perfectly acceptable (according to research carried out by BRMB for the Funeralcare Forum) there is a need to revise funerals. This does not mean disregarding what happens altogether or what has gone before, but looking instead at integrating and complementing this with modern values and beliefs.

Playwright, theatre director and ordained priest, James Roose-Evans, says in *Passages of the Soul — Rediscovering the Importance of Rituals in Everyday Life:*

'*all great faiths have precise rituals for the dying and the dead – what rituals do we have to offer to those of no specific faith or tradition? A ritual is a journey of the heart, which should lead us into the inner realm of the psyche, and ultimately, into that of the soul, the ground of our being. Rituals, if performed with passion and devotion, will enhance our desire and strengthen our capacity to live. New rituals will evolve but the ancient rituals and liturgies are also capable of rediscovery as we learn to make them our own.*'

We need good funeral ceremonies and rituals in order to understand our loss and the maelström of feelings associated with such loss. It is only then that we can accept, let go and feel our own sense of being in the new order of our world. A good ceremony illuminates the life of the person who has died. This is the last act, the final curtain, a chance to speak clearly, and when we do, we have stories and memories to give us warmth and nourishment in times of need.

preparation for a ceremony with heart and soul

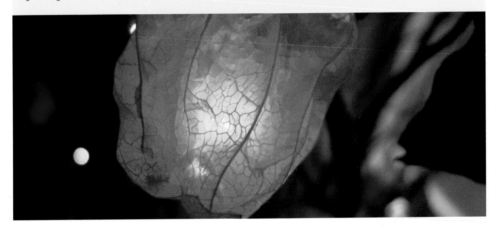

A ceremony with heart includes the passions and loves of the person who has died, and a ceremony with soul reflects their values, beliefs and spirituality. The ceremonies that work well need to reflect the beliefs and personality of the person who has died; it is about them.

When thinking about a funeral ceremony, designing it almost, it is important to discover what you want to achieve and to draw up a broad outline, to which you can then add the details. This section looks at the aims of a funeral ceremony and who can conduct it. There are down-to-earth, practical aspects to consider. To what extent do the family want to be involved in creating and running the ceremony? Family members may have very different views as to what a funeral should be like, which may also differ from the views of friends. This section explores how to deal with disagreements, and manage expectations, so that everyone feels included.

43 funeral ceremonies re-visioned

At the beginning of the twenty-first century, it is permissible to say that many of the traditional religious ceremonies have lost their power and impact for many of us, because they are out of step with contemporary thought and philosophy. At a time of crisis, the old liturgies and well-established sacred spaces provide a great sense of continuity and comfort, but less than one in five people in the UK is actively connected to a church or other religious institution.

Vibrant and relevant ceremonies, wherever they are held, manage to integrate both traditional and new, religious and secular. This is not about choosing between them, or replacing one with the other, but finding a place where they can unite.

Within a family it is very likely there will be a wide range of beliefs so a funeral ceremony that can combine the comfort of the old and be inspired by the new is possible and often appropriate to commemorate the life of the person who has died.

A ceremony which reflects the diversity of spiritual views and beliefs of the person and their family can be put together and held by an independent funeral conductor, a friend or family member, and this would most likely be held in a non-religious location.

If you would like a ceremony in your place of religion, but also want the ceremony to include secular influences, it is always worth asking your minister what they will allow outside the normal traditional service. Some of them are quite flexible.

Crematoria are not denominated and so are available for all types of services. Most have Christian religious icons, but you can ask for these to be removed, if you wish, and bring in items which have meaning for you. The British Humanist Association provides celebrants for wholly secular services with no religious references at all. There is no law to say you have to have a minister of religion.

A family-led funeral in church – Simon's story

S, like many of us, held a complex weave of interests, including her own eclectic spirituality, with interests in yoga and Buddhism as well as respect for her Christian roots. She enjoyed Mozart and The Doobie Brothers, flamenco and Queen. She loved living in the buzz of London, but had a need for nature and the countryside. She worked in medical science, but was also a trained herbalist. She enjoyed both meditation and a good night out at the pub. The blight of her life was her depression. Sadly, she committed suicide at the age of 42.

I had never organised a funeral before and depended on the services of the funeral director, but I was determined to organise the ceremony itself. Her funeral needed to reflect her personality, but also be accessible to her parents, and her many friends and colleagues who were in shock. It was held in the church in which she had been baptised and married. The non-stipendiary priest, who had known her, was happy for the service to be broad in its scope and for others to lead parts of it.

We sang hymns but also a song she loved. We read from Kahlil Gibran's *The Prophet* and some modern poetry. A dramatically performed piece by Ben Okri about a flamenco dancer, in terror preparing for her dance in which she risks everything to 'stamp the dampness from her soul', brought in thoughts about depression and suicide. Family, friends and colleagues spoke about what S meant to them and wished her well. We had prayers. At the end, we released a homing pigeon as a symbol of her journey back to her spiritual home, wherever that may be.

By combining different spiritual and secular beliefs, by including her suicide, we captured her essence, at the same time as giving comfort and inspiration to those who mourned her. The atmosphere of the service was one of celebration of her as a person, as well as reflecting the sadness and futility of a life cut off in its prime.

44 four aims

When starting to think about what sort of funeral you want and how to make it happen it is useful to keep four important aims in mind. These can provide a guide when you are trying to sort out the order of readings and music with the family and/or the funeral conductor. They are:

1. To give the bereaved comfort and an opportunity to reflect on and share their loss.
2. To acknowledge the life of the person in the world in a truthful way and give thanks for that life in its richness and diversity. The person will have meant different things to different people.
3. To acknowledge the loss and ask for the safe transition of the spirit or soul into whatever is believed to lie beyond.
4. To give the bereaved the hope and inspiration to resume their lives in the knowledge that things have irretrievably changed.

How much time or emphasis you give to each of these depends on the circumstances of the person's death and your own personal preference. However, the four aims seem to hold true for someone who dies in their twenties or nineties or for the death of a child. Life's value is not measured in years. The bereaved always need comfort; the life has always had an impact to be acknowledged and remembered; the spirit has its next journey to make.

45 remember who the ceremony is about

The best ceremonies respect, honour and reflect the person who has died. If you really want to create a personal funeral let the person's passions and loves direct how the ceremony will be. Think about how they lived their life, their interests and hobbies, profession and philosophy. If you can filter the choices of words, music and poetry for the ceremony through their eyes, no one at the funeral will doubt to whom they are saying goodbye.

46 a family-run ceremony

There is no requirement to have any type of
official to lead the ceremony and, though it might
be a daunting prospect, you can do it yourselves. It
is easier to do this if the family group is cohesive
and the number of participants few.

'R's funeral was a collective effort, at which four of
his close family each spoke about a stage of his life
when they knew him best. Everyone had a
ceremony sheet and took their cue from the
previous person. Someone was appointed to make
sure that the pieces of music started at the right time
and another led the words said by everyone at the
committal but, apart from that, the ceremony could
proceed at its own pace. The informality allowed
people to take their time when overcome by grief as
they were speaking. Gaps did not seem awkward – they gave time for emotion and
reflection. There were no time constraints within the chapel.'

In order to prepare for this type of occasion, spend time discussing and planning
the ceremony together and write it down. This can look and feel a bit like a drama
script. Then as long as everyone knows the order to follow, things should run
smoothly. If you are time constrained, appoint someone as timekeeper to try to
keep it on schedule. The closeness of the family group provides a safe environment,
allowing everyone to feel and express their emotions. If you are in any doubt about
the cohesiveness of the family it is better to find a funeral conductor.

47 **the funeral conductor**

If you have no specific faith or tradition, an independent funeral conductor will act as a conduit through whom to express your views and beliefs in a ceremony.

The majority of funeral services are carried out within the auspices of the religious beliefs of the person who has died, and follow a traditional pattern. Because a recognised member of the clergy, religious minister or registrar is not legally required to hold a funeral, you can choose a conductor of your own, who can be a friend or relation of the person or a professional.

An independent funeral conductor can be very flexible, understanding and supportive as the family moves through the process of making preparations for the funeral. He or she will work closely with them to understand the life and relationships of the person who has died and to explore and shape the type of ceremony the family envisage. Shewill hold the focus of the ceremony on the unique life and death of the person. At a time when the family is in a state of despair and dependence, the conductor offers the security and inspiration of beautiful, heartfelt words, music and ritual as well as hope where none seems to exist. As Tony Walter comments in his book *Funerals And How To Improve Them:* 'Celebrants must know that, while remaining genuine, they are playing a part. They must acknowledge despair, but not give in to their own despair.'

A skilled funeral conductor will be able to structure a ceremony which provides a safe environment in which mourners can mourn. He will be there to direct the ceremony, and is available to read poems, deliver an account of the person and lend support to those participating.

See page 193 for a list of places to find funeral conductors.

A funeral conductor may:
- sit with someone who is dying to listen to their story and their requests
- help the family create the funeral ceremony
- create the funeral ceremony on behalf of the family
- help the family choose poems, texts and music
- liaise with the funeral director over the organisational details of the ceremony
- write, or help you to write, the eulogy
- help you choose a ceremonial venue
- conduct the ceremony
- organise ceremony sheets

48 **when a child dies**

The death of your child turns your world completely upside down, it is against the natural order of things. A child is your hope for the future; your child should not be dead while you are still alive. You feel unhinged by the unimaginable intensity of your feelings, the loss is absolute and you may feel as though you are going mad by trying to make sense out of nonsense. You may rage and scream against the world, you may shut down completely, you may be in complete denial, you may suffer intolerable physical pain, there is no right or wrong way to grieve or experience your loss. There is no limit on your grief, apparently normal everyday things may trigger in you extreme reactions, and your relationships may be tested to the extreme. Nobody fully recovers from the death of a child; they adjust to it as best they can.

A child's funeral will be organised during a period of raw emotion whether the death was unexpected or anticipated (as in terminal illness). You will be offered, and you will need to accept a lot of help. If a child has been cared for by a children's hospice, the family is very well looked after by the bereavement support team – physically, emotionally and also with the practicalities of arranging a funeral.

If a child dies very young, you can still prepare a eulogy. You can talk about their characteristics, what they liked, some stories and memories from their life, the impact they had on others. A eulogy does not have to be a catalogue of achievements. The value of a life is not measured by its length. The short life of a baby or child can touch many people, making them reassess their own lives. In our work, we met parents who came to terms with the short life of their little boy, who had a life-limiting genetic condition. They accepted that this was, simply, his pre-ordained time here and that his shortened life was perfect for him.

The friends of a teenager will need a role to help them to express their grief. It is very shocking for them to lose one of their own generation so prematurely. Some may wish to see the body, in order for the reality of the death to sink in, or may offer music, poetry, readings and memories at the celebration and others will offer their talents to decorate or even to carry the coffin.

Whether it is the funeral for a young child or a teenager it is important to make the funeral appropriate to their generation, with poetry, music, readings, decoration, etc.

Doris Stickney explains death to young children in *Water Bugs and Dragonflies*, a book that could also be appreciated by adults.

49 **include everyone**

When you have decided to arrange a personal funeral, which you hope will be memorable on someone's behalf, it is possible that not all the family are going to understand why, how or indeed *if* this should be done.

Death brings people much closer to their own personal issues of what is right and what is wrong and these values are easily projected not only onto the person who has died but also onto the person who is taking responsibility for the funeral arrangements. If you are the one taking responsibility it is useful to remember this.

Ask members of the family for their own thoughts and contributions to the ceremony, but remember that the character, wishes and belief system of the person who has died are key when deciding what to include; the family might need to have this explained and clarified.

For example, throughout his adult life T had found wisdom and inspiration from Native American teachings. He died an unexpected death and when his sister came from North America for the funeral she expected a Church of England service. The result was a ceremony including Native American prayers, a Christian blessing and a slightly amended hymn spoken by everyone at his graveside. Many present commented that it had been a fitting tribute to him, even the funeral directors were sufficiently moved to comment on the sincerity and emotional depth of the service.

Very often, once initial resistance has been overcome, the response to a more personal ceremony is positive. If the ceremony captures the essence of the person, most people are moved by the experience and enjoy any less conventional elements.

Fear no more the heat o' th' sun,
Nor the furious winter rages;
Thou thy worldly task hast done,
Home art gone, and ta'en thy wages:
Golden lads and girls all must,
As chimney-sweepers, come to dust.

Cymbeline Act 4 scene 3
William Shakespeare

50 when the family does not agree

Our family groups are now flung far and wide. We have been encouraged to follow personal careers wherever they may lead us and often little regard is paid by family members to the integrity of the family and its support system. This living and growing apart may not obviously bother us too much, but at times of illness and death it can be a different story, and, radically different and painful points of view may emerge.

Observations made recently by a relative faced with a deep family divide sum up the dilemma of organising a funeral ceremony today: 'Funerals used to be very simple. We used to have a ceremony in church or in the crematorium followed by a burial or a cremation and that was that. No difficult decisions to be made.'

But you may be faced with those difficult decisions, which could turn into bitter arguments. If the person who has died has expressed some wishes, try to keep as close to these as possible, even if it means considering adaptation and compromise. When views are very polarised try to minimise the hurt by considering who is going to suffer most in the long term; is it the estranged brother and sister who share a complicated emotional history with their sibling or is it the group of friends with whom she spent the last five years of her life? Another course of action is to find a mediator, perhaps one of the executors, an old friend of the family, a funeral adviser or guardian.

The best solution of all is to make known your own funeral wishes prior to death, in case of a family disagreement. There is no obligation on those left behind to follow these wishes but if you write them down and set some money aside it may help a great deal. There is no legal hierarchy between next of kin, relatives and executors. If at all possible things need to be sorted out by negotiation.

a beautiful ceremony space

When the bustle of everyday life is put aside for a short while and we step into a beautiful space that has been prepared for a ritual, we are able to connect to what is important, what is sacred. The decoration of the space can be as important a part of the ceremony as the words and music. If a group has gathered to set the scene thoughtfully and appropriately it is possible for a deeper and more meaningful ceremony to occur. The desired effect is, that there is no doubt that you are stepping into a ritual space, which is different and apart from our everyday world. Most venues can be decorated in some way:

- if you want to decorate the crematorium it is best to book a double time slot
- keep the decoration representative of the person
- do not try to organise it on your own. Ask for help in planning and setting up
- friends and family will often want to participate but need to be asked
- you can do a lot within a small budget
- many more ideas on decoration are in *The Dead Good Funerals Book*

51 **decoration**

L talked extensively to us about her own funeral arrangements eighteen months before she died. She was adamant that she did not wish the ceremony to be held in the crematorium, but perhaps in a pub or in a hall. When the time came we found a pub with a big function room and a private entrance opening out onto a terrace garden. It was the perfect setting. Perhaps it is important to mention here that the space needs to feel safe, a place where people can let go and emerge feeling reconstructed.

The room itself needed preparing: it was aired and incense sticks were burned to clear the pub atmosphere; the dark oak panelling was fringed with swathes of sky blue fabric and the beams decorated with foliage. The entrance became an archway of foliage, white flowers and candles. The corners of the room were piled high with plants and teddy bears, she was passionate about both: flowers and plants surrounded her willow coffin on its bier in the middle of the room. Her three favourite bears were placed on top of her coffin.

The rectangular room allowed the seating to be arranged on all sides of the coffin. Friends helped decorate and move furniture, others delivered plants on loan, still more helped to take everything away again at the end of the day. The temporary transformation of a public room into a sacred space for a private ceremony was very successful and spoke directly of L and the things she held close to her heart.

52 flowers as a potent symbol

For centuries, across cultures, the uplifting simplicity and beauty of flowers at a time of grief has been of great comfort. The strength of their beauty has the power to convey feelings that cannot be spoken at a time of emotional distress. Flowers are a symbol of the fragility of our life on earth and a poignant reminder of our interrelationship with nature. A single stem, or a simple posy gathered by a child and placed on top of the coffin has a special eloquence; Princess Diana's children placed lilies on her coffin.

The standardisation of flower choice for funeral pieces has made ordering very easy but has eroded meaning, passion and creativity. It is not possible to read intimate messages from conveyor-belt flowers.

Flowers are a potent symbol because they connect us to the natural life cycle but we forfeit their capacity to inspire and comfort us, when all year round, the same flower pieces using a restricted variety of flowers blind us to the beauty and freshness of seasonal flowers and personally crafted tributes.

D's body was brought back to the UK from Greece where he had died on holiday. His widow asked for the coffin flowers to imitate a Greek hillside in spring. A rocky landscape complete with bleached wood, anemones, irises, grape hyacinths and aromatic herbs was devised by the florists, which was met with heartfelt thanks and appreciation from his family.

An elderly Quaker gentleman who was a devoted organic vegetable grower died. His relatives requested a plate of organic vegetables to place on top of the coffin. After the ceremony at the crematorium the plate of 'veg' and his cap took pride of place at the Quaker Meeting House where friends and family met to remember him.

53 flowers as a soothing, sensual memory

Fresh, vibrant flowers on top of the coffin can be a point of focus during the emotionally difficult ritual of saying goodbye, and as time passes may become a soothing and inspirational memory. Snowdrops and narcissi set in a woodland scene of catkins and pussy willow in spring; a mass of colourful full-blown scented roses with herbs in summer; an abundance of fruits and flowers, blackberries, crab apples, echinacea in autumn; or the exotic blooms of amaryllis with winter berries and foliage in the colder months. You can be creative as you like, whether you organise them yourself or find a florist to help you.

A thing of beauty is a joy for ever
Its loveliness increases; it will never
Pass into nothingness; but still will keep
A bower quiet for us, and a sleep
Full of sweet dreams, and health, and quiet breathing.
Therefore, on every morrow, are we wreathing
A flowery band to bind us to the earth,
Spite of despondence, of the inhuman dearth
Of noble natures, of the gloomy days.
Of all the unhealthy and o'er-darkened ways
Made for our searching: yes, in spite of all,
Some shape of beauty moves away the pall
From our dark spirits...

From Endymion
John Keats

54 **the florist**

Selecting flowers for a funeral is not something you do everyday, indeed you may never have done so. If flowers are important to you, try to find a florist who is sympathetic and happy to listen to you rather than one who simply encourages you to choose flowers from a catalogue. Say right from the beginning you would like something individual or creative. Some florists will be very willing and able to work with this. You do not need to use conifer, carnations or chrysanthemums. You can choose whatever you like best as long as you give the florist enough time to order.

If they are handled carefully funeral flowers do not need cellophane. Cellophane obscures and distorts the flowers through the film, and may also mist up due to temperature changes. It is an environmental nuisance and definitely should be avoided for green burial sites. Let the florist know your views on this.

There are no rules surrounding flower pieces for funerals. Most funeral directors appreciate the flowers being easy to carry, transport and display, and compact enough to fit in the hearse, if that is the chosen vehicle. If the flowers are to be placed on top of the coffin in a hearse the arrangement can only be 30–35 cm (12 in) high. Talk to the florist about:

• your budget
• a favourite season, fond memories and places visited
• the primary interests/occupations/ hobbies of the person who has died
• favourite flowers and foliage
• scent and colour preferences
• style: wild, contemporary or traditional
• including flowers and foliage from the person's garden

55 organising the flowers yourself

It is lovely to organise and arrange as many of the flowers as you feel able to.

- a good way to involve the family is to form a group to organise the flowers the day before the funeral. This brings people together to chat, tell stories and share memories
- using a mixture of flowers from the florist with garden flowers and foliage helps you with colour and impact
- pick garden flowers early in the morning. Leave to drink in a bucket of water in a cool shady place for twenty-four hours and they will remain fresh. Wild flowers are more delicate
- the flower pieces do not have to look perfect. You will foster a sense of connection to the person if you do what feels natural to you and gives you pleasure
- flat-backed sprays of flowers are easy to carry and put into position

If you have early access to the venue you can prepare the space in advance. If time is tight at the crematorium it is fine to take the flowers in with you and place them on the coffin or around the room.

If the funeral is held in church at a time when no flowers are allowed, Advent and Lent, you need to talk to the vicar to make sure some flowers will be allowed.

56 weaving flowers into the coffin

In the crematorium the coffin is traditionally placed at a distance from the mourners. Often people respond very positively to the chance of moving close to the coffin, and if it is a woven coffin, bamboo or willow for example, they can place a flower stem into the weave. Encouraging people to gather together like this helps to break the formality of the occasion and brings feelings of comfort and inclusivity for those who want to participate.

Roses, tea tree, camellia, eryngium thistle, heather and herbs are good choices because they have woody stems which are not too thick.

The weave of a coffin is close and stiff so flowers with thick fleshy stems are not suitable. These types of flowers are better placed on top.

57 where do all the flowers go?

It is easy to understand why the family wish for the funeral flowers to be delivered to the nursing home or hospice, but it is difficult to see what enjoyment the very obvious sympathy arrangements bring. If you order a sheath of pretty flowers and foliage on long stems less commonly associated with funerals, the arrangements can be taken apart and the flowers displayed elegantly and cheerfully in vases of water. They will be more appreciated like this.

Thoughtfully chosen and arranged coffin sprays can be taken home from the crematorium. Ask someone prior to the ceremony to do this for you, either a friend or the funeral director.

The blossoms weep dew or fill their cups with mist droplets as if they were sad and lamenting. They can endure sharp frost and snow. They announce Spring's earliest beginning. Shyly blushing they turn their laughing faces away from the sun. Then they open wide, before they start to fade. The buds are like strings of pearls, protected from cold and chilling mist, well-sheltered until spring summons them to open. Then come the bees and butterflies, and finally the wind. So is their life-cycle fulfilled, but from the moment when they open to when they fade away they radiate love.

A treatise on cherry blossom, Hua-Kuang

58 making an entrance

Decorating an entrance is a simple way to let everyone know they are entering a special place. Use flowers and foliage, fairy lights, ribbons, fabrics, decorated tools such as hoes or garden forks, even a decorated coatstand with someone's hat, coat and an umbrella would highlight an entrance or exit.

A little girl died and her funeral was held in the local church. A group from her school constructed an archway from wire to fit inside the doorway of the church and decorated it with bright pink roses and foliage. It looked beautiful and as everyone arrived for the ceremony they had to step through it, leaving no doubt that they were entering a very special time and space.

59 **candles**

Placing and lighting candles is a very effective and easy way to make a space different and special and is used extensively by most religions. The lighting and extinguishing of a flame is a simple and direct metaphor for life and death.

A very simple and effective ceremony can be made by lighting candles or nightlights as the ceremony begins, maybe one to represent each year, or decade, the person lived.

As the ceremony proceeds, perhaps during a period when people are sharing their thoughts about the person who has died, extinguish these one by one, symbolising the passing of the many aspects of the person.

Before the very last one is extinguished, a new candle is lit from this, representing the stage of transition. Make this a large candle, different to those put out. For example, it could be coloured if the others are white.

• make sure that the use of candles is permitted where the ceremony is to be held
• remember to place candles in holders or on plates to prevent damage to surfaces
• church candles, which burn in and do not drip are a good choice; they also burn for a long time
• groups of church candles, three or five, at different heights look good
• clusters or long lines of nightlights are very effective but make sure they are in holders or on trays, etc.
• use a taper rather than matches to light a lot of candles during a ceremony

60 **using photos**

Although you may have a portrait of the person who has died, you can extend this by creating a montage of photos. By doing this you can personalise the ceremony with immediate effect. If you identify the other characters in the photos it will help to stimulate lots more memories and stories and become a talking point. The montage can be put near the entrance, so everyone can see it as they come in, or near the coffin if you think people will have enough time to move around before or during the ceremony.

A photo montage works well for a ceremony held in most venues and you can take it with you to the gathering afterwards.

61 **scent**

You can enhance the atmosphere of a room using flowers, herbs, incense and candles. It is a very simple way to suggest a ritual space. Be sensitive with your choice of scent and how much you use. The sense of smell has a very immediate and direct impact on people, and it is easy to overdo it. A lifelong aversion can arise from the smell of lilies, narcissi, jasmine and so on because the scent was too overpowering and associated with death.

• woody, spicy, herbal and mossy essences are good. Floral essences may be too sweet and powerful
• natural essences are best, synthetic sprays are not suitable
• use incense sticks, essentials oils in a burner, or scented candles

On the other hand, masses of the same scent, in this case scented roses, blending with the ancient aromas of a church, brought a special significance to the family attending the funeral ceremony of an elderly lady.

An old lady died in the middle of June, at the time of year her garden was overflowing with scented roses. Her daughter thought that the most appropriate flowers for the top of her coffin would be the roses she loved dearly. The day before the funeral she arrived with five buckets of blooms in all shapes, colours and scents. Using a wire and moss frame and lots of foliage the florist created a six foot spray for the length of the coffin. The scent in the church was wonderful and connected everyone to the old lady. After her burial the family took the piece home and enjoyed the flowers until they too faded away.

62 **sound**

Ensure you find the right recordings to play and give clear instructions to whoever is operating the sound system. Consider using 'ambient' sounds other than music and singing to create an atmosphere.

A funeral ceremony for a lady who loved to sit and listen to birdsong in her garden was held in the local church. Her family decided that it would be lovely for everyone to listen to a few minutes from a tape of British birdsong. They were startled when loud screeching and whistling echoed round the church accompanied by a commentary on birds of the Amazon basin. This continued for about five minutes because the operator did not recognise his mistake and nobody dared say anything. Afterwards everyone concluded that she would have loved alarming everyone and had probably organised it herself!

Even seagulls could be evocative for a sailor or a lover of the sea.

63 **light**

If you have the opportunity to think about and alter the lighting at a venue, you may be able to make a real contribution to creating a ceremonial space.

* candles have ancient associations with the church, and special times and places, and can transform an ordinary space into a ceremonial one. Place large, slow burning, church candles at entrances and near the coffin. You could open and close the ceremony by lighting and snuffing a candle, a symbol of the beginning and the end of a life. Or use the candle ritual in 59
* nightlights are easy to use and look very beautiful in groups on plates or trays. You can buy incense candles which combine both the aroma and light. Check with the venue that this is permissible within their health and safety rules
* lanterns and lamps will throw more light than the candles but can be used in similar ways, perhaps to illuminate a photo or favourite object
* electric fairy lights, either as single lines or in nets, can be very effective and especially appropriate for a ceremony for a child
* natural light can be used to back light cut outs to make different shapes and patterns in the room. This is a very economical and unique way to personalise the space. *The Dead Good Funerals Book* has many ideas on light and decorating spaces

Below: birds representing souls passing through; Photo Arts by Sabra Lawrence.

64 **dress**

When someone died the Victorians wore black, and lots of it. Nowadays, it is not so easy to choose what to wear at a funeral, if no guidelines have been set. It is assumed that smart, sombre clothes will be worn, unless advised otherwise. It is safe to say that the more formal the funeral, the greater the expectation to dress in black or dark formal clothes.

If a funeral is styled purely as a celebration of life, then bright colours may well be acceptable. Friends and family were asked to wear something glittery for the funeral of a six-year-old child. Whatever you decide, try to let people know. Once, as a funeral conductor, I was asked to wear my stripey multicoloured coat! Casual clothes often do not look out of place and for a woodland funeral you may be expected to walk down stony paths or across grass, so wear some comfortable shoes. Woodland funeral sites are often set on the side of a hill and have great views, which also means that in winter they can be bitterly cold. If you are travelling some distance, listen to the forecast before you go, or talk to someone local and be prepared for the unpredictable British weather. Hip flasks and hand warmers may serve you well.

65 **sitting in the round**

Rearranging the seating from the usual rows of chairs helps to create a different environment for a funeral ceremony.

Usually a funeral is held with the coffin on the catafalque at the front and everyone in rows looking forwards at it. Consequently, they are unable to see each other and may have a poor view of the coffin.

Sitting in a circle around the coffin, which is placed on a low bier in the middle so that everyone has a good view of it and can see each other as well, creates an intimate and communicative environment. This works well even if you need more than one circle in order to accommodate everyone, in which case you will need to leave a few gaps to pass through to the row in front. Be aware of leaving enough avenues to satisfy fire and health and safety regulations.

The circular arrangement is less 'hierarchical', and enables those participating to move around more easily and to get closer to the coffin to place a message or sprig of herbs or flowers on it. This seating arrangement increases everyone's sense of connection with the coffin and each other. It makes the ceremony feel less formal and encourages participation. Alternatively, a horseshoe shape with the coffin at the open end still enables more of those gathered to see each other.

You need to consider carefully whether or not a new seating arrangement will suit everyone. When people are very upset they may feel too exposed if asked to face others in a circle.

Changing the seating in a church or crematorium can be difficult if the seats are fixed or the person in charge is resistant to the idea. Some crematoria say this is possible and it is worth asking. Flexibility of seating is an advantage of many alternative venues.

the arrival of the coffin

Most funerals still adhere to Victorian formality. The large sombre hearse, everyone dressed in black, 'church-like' even if not taking place in a church. This suits some people, but for many it brings a remoteness they did not associate with the person who died and is alien to their personality.

Funerals can be much more informal, and in this section we look at alternative forms of transport, the involvement of family and friends in the arrival of the coffin and the impact of the arrival of the coffin.

66 **it could not be anyone else**

When N's coffin entered the ceremony with his fedora and drumsticks on it, there could be no mistaking who the coffin contained.

He goes free of the earth.
The sun of his last day sets
clear in the sweetness of his liberty.

The earth recovers from his dying,
the hallow of his life remaining
in all his death leaves.

Radiances know him. Grown lighter
than breath, he is set free
in our remembering. Grown brighter

than vision, he goes dark
into the life of the hill
that holds his peace.

He is hidden among all that is,
and cannot be lost.

extract from 'Three Elegiac Poems', Wendell Berry

67 **taking the coffin to the funeral**

When you think of transport for funerals, you probably think of the big, black hearse to transport the coffin and one or two limousines for the family. They certainly look dignified, but also rather formal and foreboding.

It is possible to hire a vintage hearse, or a stagecoach pulled by black horses with plumes, which looks dramatic. But if you want a more down-to-earth look you could see if you can find a local farmer with horses and a flat-bed cart, which you could decorate.

If you really want to be informal there is no reason why you should not drive a vehicle yourself or ask a friend to do it.

One young man arrived at the church in the organic vegetable van. If you have a large estate car or Land Rover, you can use that. People have taken the passenger seat out of a hatchback or people carrier to get the coffin in, used a VW Microbus or other leisure vehicle. We recently helped a family to process the coffin from the funeral director's premises near the central car park through the small town and down the country lanes to the burial site.

The most important factor to take into account is that the transport should be fitting to the positive character of the person who has died – not a joke or denigration.

68 timing the arrival of the coffin

Decide whether to have the coffin in the room before people arrive, or wait until everyone is settled and have the bearers process it to its resting place.

If the coffin is already in place on the catafalque, or bier, when they arrive, people have time to settle, focus or go up to it, touch it and place their flowers.

It is much more dramatic for the bearers to enter with the coffin when everyone is present and there are many occasions when this may be highly appropriate.

69 processing with the coffin

Until the 1950s, it was commonplace to process the coffin from home to the church, or the funeral director would walk in front of the hearse at least some of the way. There are still one or two that do. Processing places a funeral in its local community. Written by M remembering her friend's funeral:

> 'R's coffin was lifted to the men's shoulders outside the farmhouse; I joined the procession of family and friends filing slowly down the path, through the wooden garden gate and into the lane as the farmhouse bell tolled. A short distance down the lane, we turned left into a green path, and as we did so the deep sonorous tones of a didgeridoo drew us towards a stone bridge crossing the trout stream. Leaving the didge behind us, we wound our way up the path through the woods. When we came to the field gate, the bearers paused to allow fresh shoulders to take the weight and we could hear the faint sweet sound of a flute calling from the far side of the field. We slowly made our way down through the field towards the grave, until the song of the flute, mingled with the birdsong, announced we had arrived at R's last resting place on his beautiful farm on a glorious autumn day; just as he had wished.'

If you are to process a long way, choose a coffin that is not too heavy e.g. willow or bamboo, and remember it could rain so cardboard may not be the best choice.
• make sure the bearers are familiar with the route to be taken
• notify the local police of the time and route you wish to process

- appoint a few willing people as traffic marshals if you are going to process along streets
- An easier method of processing with the coffin is to strap it to a stretcher, which spreads the weight, allows the bearers more room, and a secure hold (see above). You can buy a bamboo stretcher from SAWD Partnership (see page 192)

70 **family and friends as bearers**

The simple act of family and friends bearing the coffin is one that is often overlooked. Overseas, and in some parts of the country, it remains part of the cultural tradition for close friends and colleagues to bear the coffin. It is a very practical and significant task that many would like the opportunity to complete.

You need six bearers, all of fairly equal height and reasonably strong. An average person's body, with the additional weight of the coffin itself, is heavy. A family who had made their own coffin out of thick planks of oak, found the load was so heavy that the bearers winced as they shouldered it. When you are making a choice of coffin, consider how far it is to be carried.

If you do not feel confident about picking up a coffin to shoulder height, it can be carried low by passing straps underneath and threaded through its handles or by the handles themselves if you order a coffin with proper, weight-bearing handles.

You may need bearers only to carry the coffin from the hearse and into the church, or crematorium, you may be planning a procession, or a burial, but in all scenarios the bearers need to be clear about their responsibilities and should discuss these closely with whoever is directing the funeral.

71 ask someone to take photos

'Thank you so much for organising someone to take photos at my aunt's funeral. They mean a great deal to me and when I look at them I remember what an amazing day it was to say goodbye to an amazing lady. It was a spring day and my favourite picture shows the beech trees surrounding the grave covered with arrangements of spring flowers. She would have loved it! Also the photos meant a huge amount to her family in Australia who could not come over. Through the pictures they have a sense of what happened and where she is now, which fills a gap until their next visit.'

- ask someone not too involved with the family
- ask someone who is used to taking pictures and will not feel awkward or shy, at the same time as being sensitive
- pictures of processing, singing, planting a tree, playing music are less intrusive than shots at emotional moments
- the place of the ceremony, flowers, trees, the grave, the funeral conductor, the location are all good shots
- if the photographer remains in one place during the ceremony they will be fairly unobtrusive
- avoid using the flash during the ceremony

the ceremony of words, music and ritual

Designing a special ceremony will keep you connected with life, and with others, at a time when you feel sad, maybe abandoned and isolated. It may even go so far as to help you to stay out of a pit of despair.

This process will help you organise your own memories, thoughts, emotions and as you work with others to understand who the person really was, you will, perhaps, gain a clearer sense of them than you ever had. You may have found the process of piecing together the constituent parts of someone's life rather extraordinary, adding to your sense of wonder not only about that person.

An added benefit of organising the components of the ceremony is the opportunity to explore your own complex feelings, and come to understand them more fully, perhaps even accept them in all their contradictions, and to know yourself better. The process of choosing and co-ordinating the words, music and imagery means you are able to describe and honour the person you love. In doing so, you will have achieved something appropriate and powerful which will help others to come to terms with the death. Moreover, you have come face to face with your own loss and, even if it does not seem like it at the time, you have started the process of coming to terms with it.

Children feel the importance of choosing a song, story or some words for the ceremony. It would not matter if it is a nursery rhyme as long as it gives a sense of connection and involvement. Older children appreciate making a contribution to the funeral of a close relative or friend, which they may write themselves.

The points in this section describe choices to be made about music and words.

The funeral ceremony contains elements of ritual, which is well described by James Roose-Evans in his book *Passages of the Soul:*

'A ritual is not to be confused with ceremonial, although ceremonial is a part of ritual. Ceremonial is concerned with the externals, varying arrangements of text, flowers, movement and music. If the externals are arranged appropriately and carefully they can set the scene for transformation to occur... Ritual works on two levels, that of the psychological and that of the spiritual, and sometimes both coincide. A ritual can resolve, at a deeper level than the intellect, some inner conflict, thereby releasing the individual from a psychological block.'

In grief, a block may include disbelief, despair, guilt and anger, but a special ceremony can help by encompassing openness and space. It is difficult to describe, but when a ceremony is more personal, less structured and unhurried, it is then that a feeling of beauty may occur and inner conflicts begin to be resolved.

DO NOT STAND AT MY GRAVE

Do not stand at my grave and weep;
I am not there. I do not sleep.
I am a thousand winds that blow.
I am the diamond glints on snow.
I am the sunlight on ripened grain
I am the gentle autumn's rain.
When you awaken in the morning's hush,
I am the swift uplifting rush
Of quiet birds in circled flight.
I am the soft stars that shine at night.
Do not stand at my grave and cry;
I am not there. I did not die.

Anon

72 the flow of the ceremony

The funeral conductor bears much responsibility for the pace of the ceremony as she directs it. The words, the music, and the ritual guide the thoughts and emotions of the mourners from intimacy and belonging, to the grief and finality of death back to life, hope and love.

How you arrange the elements of the ceremony will have a significant bearing on the flow. A tapestry of voices speaking and singing, the playing of music and readings will bring emotional depth and significance. When you have selected all the pieces for the ceremony, organise them into a 'script'. Below is an outline to help you with the order of ceremony. A ceremony sheet, that everyone can refer to, will help enormously (see page 128).

- music to enter
- opening words
- words on life and death
- the eulogy
- the committal
- closing words
- music to leave

Each part of the ceremony includes its own words, readings, music, and ritual as outlined in this section.

73 the order of ceremony sheet

A ceremony sheet that has been prepared with care and attention helps to focus everyone when they arrive, and gives them a good idea of the ceremony they are to follow. When you organise the flow of the ceremony, you will be listing the sequence of events, poetry, eulogy, readings, music, committal, as you wish them to happen and this will form the basis of the ceremony sheet.

It is helpful and interesting to know the words of a poem, a song or a hymn, especially if being asked to sing. If you do not think you have room to print out all the words, give good references so that the poem may be looked up afterwards.

An elegant ceremony sheet with a personal touch can be prepared quite easily on a home computer, and either printed at home on good quality card, white or coloured, or taken to your local copy shop on a disc. Choose an appropriate picture for the cover; a photo of the person, perhaps when they were younger, their garden, a holiday scene, wildlife photo, favourite building, child's drawing or particular icon. This makes it a personal document, specifically to illuminate the life of the person who has died, and a tool for the ceremony.

Remember to give a sheet to the funeral director, the person in charge of the music and anyone else with organisational responsibility.

You can download a ceremony sheet template from www.funeraladvisers.org.uk.

Suggestions for the ceremony sheet

To make a four-sided A5 sheet that prints on both sides of an A4 sheet, which you then fold, arrange the pages in the order of back page, front page, left-hand middle page, right-hand middle page.

Layout cover should include picture, name, date of birth and death, time and location of funeral/burial.

Choose an A4 lightweight card (100–160gsm), white or coloured.

List the flow of events including:

* songs or hymns to be sung and poems or prose to be read and by whom
* name the musical pieces and who is playing
* at the end invite people to the gathering afterwards

Include details of any organisations to whom donations may be made.

Print a few more than you think is necessary for the day to cover the unexpected arrivals and send to those who are unable to attend.

Carefully check for correct spelling, especially of names, and preview before printing.

74 **opening words**

The purpose of the opening words is to welcome everyone and focus them on the proceedings. When people are disorientated by grief and they enter an unexpected space with an unknown funeral conductor this will help them to feel accepted and included.

   The conductor needs to introduce herself, explain her role and tell everyone why they are here and what is going to happen. This helps to give the ceremony structure and safe boundaries where people can participate and let go of their feelings. Two examples are:

> 'Good morning to you all. My name is M and I am an independent funeral conductor. I have been asked by the family to lead the ceremony this morning. We are here to perform the sad act of saying goodbye to G, and also to celebrate her life and give thanks for all she gave to each of you, her relations, friends and colleagues.
>
>   We will listen to two readings and sing a song G loved and which her father used to sing to her. You have the words on your ceremony sheets. A short tribute will be read, but central to this ceremony today will be time for each of you to reflect on and say about her anything you feel moved to say. In this way G will be remembered and appreciated for who she was.
>
>   We will then commit G's body to the fire of cremation and end with a few closing words of comfort and inspiration.'

> 'Good morning everyone, we have come to say our last goodbyes to T, whose death at fifty seven has left a deep sense of sadness, loss and shock

amongst many of his family and friends.

   According to some of his friends, T was a complex, diverse man – a free spirit and radical thinker – his own person, soulful and sensitive. He loved music, so we will keep words to a minimum and let music speak for him. However, we begin with some words, which T loved and which, if anything could, seem an appropriate epitaph…'

Life is eternal and love is immortal, and death is only the horizon, and the horizon is nothing save the limit of our sight.

Rossiter Raymond (1840–1918)

75 **a moment of grace**

You cannot schedule a moment of grace. You can only allow for it in case it should happen. It can arrive in many, many different ways. Here are a few:

At the end of the reading there was a pause and quite spontaneously the reader invited everyone to go up to F's coffin to see the decoration. As the small group came closer together they felt an extraordinary sense of unity in their sadness.

Instead of reciting a well-known poem, as scheduled, the granddaughter spontaneously spoke her own poem full of memories of herself as a little girl with her grandmother. In the poignancy of her images everyone could feel again the love and care that filled her grandmother's life.

As the funeral conductor was talking about R's love of her garden, a shaft of sunlight illuminated the flowers on her coffin.

The wrong piece of music was played, but it turned out to be entirely appropriate because it made everyone laugh and think of M and how he would have loved it anyway.

A woman speaking at the funeral of her greatest friend said: 'The thing about P was that she loved everybody – even the most awful people.' Everyone instantly knew what she meant and the gathering was suffused with love, laughter and sadness.

Gathered around a grave in open woodland, a hundred people were taught a simple song in praise of nature in the round. As confidence grew, the voices swelled until everyone felt that the trees and the birds had heard and were in unison.

The family gathered at midday by the graveside to place M's ashes in her husband's grave. Just as they were about to start, a magnificent dog fox trotted right past the group. M loved foxes and had joked to her son a few months previously about 'coming back' as one.

A small family group were gathered at the graveside on a spring day in a woodland burial ground. As part of the very simple ceremony, the daughter read a love letter written from her father to her mother when they were young lovers. In that reading, she and her brother understood the love that they had been born into and which had sustained them throughout their lives.

76 **music**

You need not feel bound by traditional, or popular, musical choices for funerals; you can choose music, songs and hymns which are significant to the life of the person who has died. In a traditional religious ceremony, the music has its allotted spaces and generally adheres to a well-known selection of hymns and songs which are appropriate and comforting. For a modern, secular ceremony, your choice can be as eclectic as the life you are celebrating. A mixture of traditional and personal pieces can be woven together, particularly bearing in mind the different generations attending, with various expectations. Music for a ceremony can be recorded, performed live or everyone singing together.

The emotional significance of certain pieces of music can affect your choices. Memories and associations are easily made if you choose from the dead person's favourite musician, songwriter or composer. The music does not have to be funereal. 'Hey Mr Tambourine Man' was sung lustily and captured the tone of one funeral recently held in a crematorium and memories came flooding back when a strong voice led everyone in an open-air rendition of 'Somewhere over the Rainbow' beside a woodland grave.

Music evokes strong emotional attachment to the person who has died and gives time for you to reflect on your relationship with them. If they choose nothing else, people will often select a piece of music for their own ceremony.

- three minutes is ample time to listen to a piece of music
- four or five pieces in a sixty-minute ceremony are probably enough, two or three in a thirty-minute ceremony
- to achieve the right sound and ambience out of doors, for example at woodland burial sites, live musicians, or a strong voice to lead the singing, are most effective

77 recorded music

You may have to rely entirely on recorded music, in which case your choice is infinite. Often the music for arriving and the music for leaving can be different in tempo.

The music for the entrance of the coffin and the funeral party is often reflective and more melancholy. The musical pieces in the middle of the ceremony may be personal, or connected to the liturgy. For leaving, more upbeat pieces help people prepare to return to their everyday lives.

- make sure there is a good sound system which is powerful enough for the room at the venue, or borrow or hire one
- even with a good-quality system it is important not to overpower everyone with music that is too loud, which can make them feel uncomfortable in the middle of the ceremony
- if you are using homemade CDs ensure that the CD player will play them. Many crematoria now request that a homemade CD arrives the day before in order for them to check that it works
- prepare a playlist for the operator of the tapes/CDs or give them a copy of the order of ceremony sheet as a music 'script'
- make sure the operator has an order of ceremony, with cues

78 **live music**

Live music is beautiful and special. It adds another dimension to the ceremony. It provides an analogy with life, each being a single and unique performance on the great stage and can be more personal.

Perhaps you would like a choir, string quartet, flamenco guitarists or Peruvian panpipes. It is worth at least trying to find whatever your imagination conjures up as being right for the funeral you are planning. John Fox wrote in the *The Dead Good Funerals Book* of a funeral where 'I'm Forever Blowing Bubbles' was played on the musical saw. He described it as the most haunting piece of music he had ever heard!

Good sources of musicians are local music colleges, churches and schools. You could ask at your local music shop or look up music teachers, music tuition, music arrangers and composers, bands and musicians in the telephone book. An organist is always available to be booked at a church or crematorium.

At the funeral of an elderly lady whose life and career had been inspired by music, the family re-formed a string quartet to play at her funeral. They had not played together for some time. They did so to great acclaim, sensing that their great aunt had heard and approved their efforts. A few weeks later L observed 'I was so nervous it was unbelievable, but I was determined to get through it, and, amazingly, we did.'

79 an evocative lone instrument

There is something particularly evocative about a lone instrument being played live before, or during, a funeral. We all know, deep down, that we go out of this world alone, and the single instrument symbolises that, as well as the unique beauty of the person.

Particularly effective single instruments are the pipes, flute, trumpet, saxophone, organ, violin, viola and cello. They are all capable of giving a soulful sound.

The solo voice is also a lone instrument and can carry the fullest range of human emotion. A friend with a good voice, or someone from the local choral society, may be very pleased to help.

- if musicians are to play at the graveside make sure they are on firm ground and give them shelter from the elements if the weather is poor
- it may be difficult for close family members to play, but do not dissuade them if that is really what they want to do and they can draw deeply on their abilities
- ask professionals, they are often very honoured to play and often available because most of their work is in the evening
- make sure you have agreed the fees with professional musicians beforehand; £100 for attendance of a single musician is average

80 **singing together**

Singing together is a unifying and moving experience at a funeral. It helps to rally people, especially if it is an uplifting song. Giving voice to a song is a way to give voice to grief and helps to release pent-up feelings. The challenge is to find songs with which most of those present will at least be familiar, and had significance for the person who has died.

Well-known hymns are frequently turned to as songs of choice. They are traditional and comforting and most people will recognise the tunes and enjoy singing them or struggle through. Remember to book the organist at the church or the crematorium.

It is fine to sing along to a CD, which provides the music and it is helpful if there is a strong leading voice to follow. Most crematoria and churches have a facility to play CDs. If you choose an alternative venue, check you have a sound system that is up to the job. Make sure everyone has a copy of the words, if not the music. Keep to relatively simple songs. 'Bohemian Rhapsody' might seem like a good idea, but could turn out to be tricky.

Alternatively, you can ask the organist or pianist if she knows the song you want to sing, then find someone with a strong voice who is willing to lead it. This really helps. It feels very discouraging when a song is sung weakly. The reason is usually lack of confidence, so someone to lead the singing, who might act as conductor too, makes all the difference. If you are singing outside, ask the group to stand close together.

'Family and friends were welcomed into every possible corner of the church. K, a much-loved, and talented young mother had died, and the community had come to say their goodbyes. As a tribute to his friend, J, a local music teacher, wrote a short song which could be sung by everyone. He played it through a few times and encouraged all to join in. Within five minutes, the church was resounding to a beautiful three-part song, composed to honour the life and inspiration of K and sung for her by those who loved her.'

81 powerful and poetic words

The ancient liturgies, worn smooth by centuries of repetition, are the glue of traditional religious ceremony and can provide great comfort. If you are writing your own ceremony, secular poems and beautiful words can bring a fusion of soul and spirit, a poignancy and an intimacy with the life of the person who has died. Also, you may include your own choice of poetry into a traditional ceremony to personalise the ceremony.

For He knows of what we are made:
He remembers we are but dust.
Our days are like the grass,
We flourish like a flower of the field:
When the wind goes over it, it is
     gone:
and its place will know it no more

        extract from Church of England
        Funeral Service, Common Worship

Antidotes to Fear of Death

Sometimes as an antidote
To fear of death,
I eat the stars.

Those nights, lying on my
   back,
I suck them from the
   quenching dark
Till they are all, all inside
   me,
Pepper hot and sharp

Sometimes, instead, I stir
   myself
Into a universe still young,
Still warm as blood:

No outer space, just space,
The light of all the not yet
   stars
Drifting like a bright mist,

And all of us, and
   everything
Already there
But unconstrained by
   form.

And sometimes it's enough
To lie down here on earth
Beside our long ancestral
   bones:

To walk across the cobble
   fields
Of our discarded skulls,
Each like a treasure, like
   a chrysalis,
Thinking: whatever left
   these husks
Flew off on bright wings.

Rebecca Elson

82 choosing poetry and readings

'I want to include beautiful poetry and prose in the ceremony, but I do not know where to find it. Can you help please?' This is a very common request arising from the chaos of immediate grief. If you do not have poetry to hand, there are a number of ways to get started; the readings do not have to be funereal – personal is fine.

First of all, try to take some quiet moments and scan a few memories linked with the person who has died. Keep a note pad by your side as you remember different scenes, occasions, associations, books and writers they loved. These notes will help to jog your memory, or inform someone else you have asked to help you to do a little research into the readings.

If choice overwhelms you when you are looking through anthologies, the notes will help to bring you back to the essence of the person and the ceremony you are planning for them.

- ask family and friends for assistance and suggestions
- ask your funeral adviser, guardian, or conductor for selections to browse
- look for edited poetry selections available at good book stores
- there are several good poetry sites on the internet
- ask if anyone in the family would like to write a poem
- use the words of a favourite song as a poem
- see page 197 for a list of poetry books and anthologies

83 words on life and death

When creating new rituals, there is the opportunity to state quite clearly the beliefs of the person who has died. These personalised rituals are necessary because many people do not have a fixed faith or religion, but may have collected truths from different spiritual paths and philosophies over the years. Conversely, they may not necessarily believe in anything. The point is not to be judgmental, but to contexture and reflect the truth of the person's beliefs, values and spiritual awakenings. It is, after all, a unique funeral and the family and friends will be able to recognise the person spoken about as the one who has died. For example:

> 'K. described herself as agnostic. She saw death as an unknown quantity, not ruling out the possibility of heaven, an ongoing journey, or that the end of this life might be just that, the end.
>
> So we could see K's death as her living soul being set free from her body, which had grown old and weary, perhaps to continue its journey into another life, perhaps to sit with God in heaven and be reunited with her husband, perhaps simply to come to rest as she is returned to the elements in the cycle of nature. We do not know the answer. We only know that everything that is born, dies. You will each have your own thoughts on this. Whatever the outcome, she lives on in our hearts and memories.'

84 **preparing a eulogy**

The eulogy (literally good words), or account of the person's life, is likely to be delivered by the funeral conductor or someone who knows the person who has died, but is not so close that they are unable to speak because of emotion. If you are the next of kin of the person who has died, you may want to write all or part of the eulogy and give it to someone to say on your behalf, or, if you want to say it yourself, have someone on standby to help you should you find it too difficult on the day.

This recounting of the life story of the person who has died is central to any funeral. It will be the last time the person who has died takes centre stage in such close company, and it helps everyone to say goodbye if the telling of this unique story can be told with honesty and respect.

Through the life story, everyone present can feel connected to the person who has died at this time of loss. If it tells of specific events and traits, it will bring the person back into everyone's minds, helping them to remember details, the voice, manner and qualities as well as interests. Remember also to place the person in his or her family, friendships, work and community groups. Everyone present will have different associations and will feel included in the group, especially if they are mentioned by name, and they identify the role they played in the life that is being described. By being included, they will be able to say farewell.

Before you start to write, take some time to think or find out about the whole life of the person. Create a 'map' of the various different aspects of their life, listing significant people, achievements, what they loved doing, their values and beliefs. If you do not know the person well, you could speak to several people and find out about everyday things like their favourite music, sense of humour, colour, film, book, or most-used phrase to help you get a rounded view of their personality. Find out about the challenges and difficulties they faced. The eulogy is often fascinating because it reveals aspects of the person many present did not previously know.

Talk to others, from school, work, clubs, as well as friends and relations. Fill in details on your map and collect short anecdotes from the different parts of their lives. In this way, you can increase your understanding of the person. The main elements of a eulogy are:

• **Life history** – this is a short summary of someone's life. Keep this fairly brief, or use it as the thread that runs through the eulogy. A long catalogue of events is difficult to listen to

• **Personality** – what the person was like, their values, how they saw the world, their emotional make up, characteristics, what adjectives you would use to describe them

• **Tribute** – this brings out some of the highlights in somebody's life, their impact, achievements and legacy – children, help they gave to others, how they influenced or changed lives, completed projects, acts of kindness

• **Challenges** – everyone faces difficulties in life, and these often shape who we become. If you mention briefly difficulties like broken relationships, depression or alcoholism, you create a rounded and realistic view of the person. You do not need to dwell on these too much, or say anything that would be upsetting to those closest to them

• **Memories and stories** – describe briefly some specific memories and stories that you and others shared with them. These are often very touching and capture their personality succinctly

• **Feelings about them** – what it was like to be with them, what they meant to you

A eulogy does not need to last more than ten minutes, which will be about one thousand five hundred words. Certainly do not pad it out. If you are delivering the eulogy, rehearse it out loud more than once, and time it. One of these rehearsals should be in front of an audience, a member of the family or a friend. This way you can fine tune the eulogy, and become less dependent on your notes.

A funeral is a very emotional time. Many in the gathering may be in tears. They will not worry if you are emotional too. If you are very close to the person who died, and you want to deliver the eulogy, have someone on hand to take over if you break down and really cannot continue. It can help just to have someone standing beside you.

85 funeral conductor delivers the eulogy

If you have asked a funeral conductor to lead the ceremony, she will be experienced and prepared to deliver the life story or eulogy in the understanding that it is the uniqueness of this human life that is to be stated.

Different people remember different anecdotes and stories, and she will wish to speak to various family members in order to write and speak as comprehensively as possible. She will perform this task with discretion and sensitivity to the family. For a variety of reasons, it may be difficult to talk to all the significant people, so even a few written anecdotes from people who cannot be present are useful.

If you would like to see a transcript of the eulogy before the ceremony, ask for it because you may want to check facts or make alterations. It is also good to have a copy to keep, possibly to send to those who are unable to attend.

M was mother to five children, and when she died everyone became painfully aware of how deeply divided they had become over the years. Adding to a variety of difficulties was that one of the siblings lived in Australia and was a practising Catholic, three were Jehovah's Witnesses and one followed Celtic traditions. M had been interested in all of these things, but had not declared any specific allegiance, preferring to keep an open mind on all things spiritual. Only one of the siblings was able to talk about her mother to the funeral conductor in any depth, the rest of the information was gathered from the family via written fragments, including an important quote from the Bible. It was clear that M had enjoyed a special relationship with each of her children. In an attempt to connect, however briefly, the brothers and sisters at their mother's funeral, the funeral conductor spoke about how special these relationships were to M, and how proud she had always felt about them all, carefully naming each of them in turn.

86 speaking on behalf of the family

It is not easy to stand up at a funeral and talk about a loved one who has died. You may have in the family an experienced and confident speaker who would like to speak, or someone else may find the strength and motivation to speak.

It is important that the majority of the family should feel comfortable with whoever chooses the task. Relationships can come under a lot of pressure at the time of death, and it is often better not to expose controversy at such a sensitive time.

If nobody seems really suitable, ask the minister or a funeral conductor to speak on behalf of the family.

87 life story told by more than one person

Sometimes it is better to share talking about the person amongst a few family and friends. The advantages of this are that each individual does not need to talk for too long, and different relationships bring different perspectives. For example, a sibling will have had a different experience of the person who has died than a son or daughter or an old school or college friend.

Ask people to be time vigilant, depending on the time schedule of the ceremony. Three people, with three minutes each, could be about right for a ceremony lasting forty minutes, but too much time for one of twenty minutes.

I loved her like the leaves,
The lush green leaves of spring
That pulled down the willows
on the bank's edge where we walked
while she was of this world.

To the shimmering wide fields
hidden by the white cloud,
white as white silk scarf
she soared away like the morning bird,
hid from our world like the setting sun.

Kakinononto Hitomaro (Japan, seventh century)

88 open space for people to speak

Holding an open space, during which anyone can speak about the person who has died will really only work if you have a generous amount of time for the ceremony. It is a very lovely thing to do, and people are often surprised and moved by the generosity and humour of these tributes. Memories, anecdotes, stories, poems and friendships are momentarily re-lived and the person may appear in an entirety never glimpsed before. This can be painful and also deeply satisfying as you realise that he/she achieved things you thought were only dreams. If a celebrant is conducting the service, he will know how to hold the space, if you are managing a family-led ceremony here are a few tips on how to do it.

Introduce the open space with a short explanation, such as 'Now we are going to have some time when anyone who feels moved to speak about J may do so. It would be good to convey your own experience of J, and please keep each contribution brief so we can hear from many people. I know that S and T would like to say something, so perhaps they could begin and others follow.' The duration of an open space can be time limited or not. If it is, you will often find that the speaking will reach a natural conclusion. It is very important that nobody feels obliged to speak, but you could ensure that there are a few who are willing to do so to start things off.

If there is a long silence, ask if anyone else would like to speak before the space is closed. You could say you know that it can be difficult to speak when full of emotion, to help take away any uneasiness.

89 space for your own reflections

The words and music leading up to the saddest and most poignant part of the ceremony have been led by the funeral conductor. The time before the committal is a good time for everyone to take a minute on their own in order to prepare themselves for the time when the coffin will move out of sight for ever.

Whoever is leading the ceremony will be able to announce the quiet time, to judge when enough time has elapsed, a minute is a good guide, and then move on towards the words of the committal.

Having drunk deeply of the heaven above and felt the most glorious beauty of the day, I desire now to become lost and absorbed into the being or existence of the universe. Deep into the earth under, and high above into the sky, and further still to the sun and stars, still further beyond the stars into the hollow of space, losing thus my separateness of being to become a part of the whole.

The Story of my Heart
Richard Jeffries, 1883

90 music at the committal

You could have a few bars of music before the words of the committal, so people can gather themselves and to emphasise the importance of this event. The words of the committal may be spoken before the coffin is lowered into the grave, or is moved or hidden in the crematorium, and beautiful music played or sung as the coffin is lowered and settled or taken out of sight. A lone instrumentalist is a good choice for the occasion but do not let the music run on too long.

For what is it to die but to stand naked in the wind
and to melt into the sun?
And what is it to cease breathing but to free the breath
from its restless tides, that it may rise and expand
and seek God unencumbered?
And when the earth shall claim your limbs, then shall
you truly dance.

The Prophet
Kahlil Gibran

91 words for the committal

It is time to say the last goodbye to the body, the physical existence of the person, letting them go to whatever is believed to lie beyond this life. It is best kept reasonably formal and brief, as this is the most distressing and upsetting part of the ceremony.

This is the moment in the crematorium about which people complain more than anything else, when the curtains close around the coffin or it moves off on a conveyor belt out of sight forever. Just as chilling is to watch the coffin being lowered into the ground.

And yet it is a vital part of the process of letting go of the person. Some avoid it by leaving the coffin where it is and the mourners leaving, but if you can face it then it is worth doing because everyone knows that the person who has died has really left.

If you are writing a ceremony, you have a wide choice of last words. For example, the committal at a small gathering for a woodland funeral used words adapted from a hymn, led by a strong voice, and spoken by all; words along the theme of 'earth to earth, ashes to ashes, dust to dust' is universal; a Haiku poem, a piece from Kahlil Gibran or a short song sung by all are among many pieces worthy of consideration.

Some words for the committal:

> 'Now we are approaching the end of our ceremony and we must say goodbye to M's body. It is time to let go, to send M off to whatever lies beyond for her with our love and gratitude. We commit M's body to the earth/fire, to be returned to the natural cycle, which sustains and regenerates all life.'

For burial:

> 'We have now reached the part of the ceremony when A's body is enfolded back into the earth which nourished her for eighty years and which regenerates all life. We give her body back to the elements, its natural end. To everything there is a season, and a time to every purpose on earth – a time to be born and a time to die. We say goodbye to A's earthly body.'

or:
> 'From dust we are made and to dust we return, we commit the body of A to the earth and pray for the safe onward passage of her soul.'

For cremation:

> 'We have now reached the part of the ceremony which commits A's body to the flames, to be burned and later returned to the earth as ashes. In this way we give her body back to the elements, its natural end, and say goodbye.'

or:

> 'Earth to earth, ashes to ashes, dust to dust. We now commit A's earthly body to the fire, to be transformed back into the elements from which it came, and pray for the safe onward passage of her soul.'

92 placing and lowering the coffin

When the bearers bring the coffin to the grave, they rest it on three slats of wood placed width ways over the grave. Three straps, made from upholsterers' furniture webbing, each about 6 m (20 ft) long are put in place with one in the middle and the other two 45 cm (18 in) from each end of the coffin. The bearers need to know where to stand during the ceremony. Ask them to step back into the circle of people, if they are family and friends, or to one side if they are professional bearers and you prefer to have an uninterrupted view of the coffin and its adornments.

When the time comes to lower the coffin into the grave, the bearers can step forward following a signal from the minister or funeral conductor. Remove the flowers from the top of the coffin. Each bearer takes up one of the loose ends of the straps. They gently take the weight of the coffin and someone removes the three slats. Then, slowly, they can lower the coffin, hand over hand. It is helpful if someone stations themselves at one end of the coffin to ensure it goes in straight. Once it has come to rest at the bottom of the grave, the bearers can step back again.

At this stage everyone can be invited to throw a handful of earth onto the top of the coffin. If the earth is very claggy and wet, it can be useful to have a bucket of dry earth. If there are shovels available, those gathered will sometimes want to fill the grave completely. A tray of petals could be prepared and these thrown in.

If you need a gravedigger for a private burial, many work independently. Funeral directors, cemetery or natural burial site managers or the local vicar may be able to find one for you.

93 **closing words**

After the committal, the closing words are ones of condolence and give everyone time to take a breath and compose themselves before going back out into the world. These words also round off the ceremony and bring it to a sense of completion. You may also invite everyone back to the venue you are going to, so that they can have something to eat and drink afterwards,

The closing words may acknowledge that life will go on without the person, and although things will never be the same again, time will heal and they will continue to live on in our hearts and memories. In that sense, we have not lost them completely. Love is not changed by death. This helps to send everyone back out into the world with a sense of hope.

If there is no need to rush out after the ceremony, those who want to could stay and listen to a piece of music, sit in silence or chat until they feel ready to move.

Some closing words:

'We have been remembering with love and gratitude the life of A. She is now gone and, although life will never be quite the same again without her, she lives on in your hearts and memories and in those of many others not present today. Take comfort from each other. Talk about her as often as you wish. Allow yourself to laugh and enjoy the memories.

'Be free to allow your grief and any difficult feelings. What is done is done and only forgiveness remains. Love is not altered by death and death takes away nothing that has happened.

'It is time now to return to life. Death is often a spur to face what we need to face in our own lives, to be purposeful and kind knowing that we are all limited and part of one humanity. In all nature, after death comes renewal. May you feel inspired and hopeful, renewed by your memories of A and for having shared in her life.'

'Give thanks for S's life and all he brought to you – and to the world. He lives on in your hearts and memories. He also leaves some loose ends and unresolved, difficult issues. Be easy on yourselves and on S. What is done is done and only love and forgiveness remain. It is time now to return to life. This existence of ours is as transient as the wind-blown clouds. Use it well, inspired by S's life. As S would say…' (put in some typical words of the person who has died, for example 'lots of love', or 'take care till we meet again').

'In a little while we will be going out into the world still feeling the loss of P, but nevertheless renewed and heartened. Talk about P as often as feels right, remember what she gave to you, be inspired by the vivacity with which she led her life. Allow yourselves your grief and your joy as you turn again to life, knowing that P is fine as she continues on her journey. She is hidden among all that is and cannot be lost. We close this ceremony with some of P's favourite writings and sayings…'

94 releasing a homing pigeon or balloons

A moving way to end a ceremony is to release a homing pigeon, symbolising the ongoing journey of the soul. If you would like to do this contact Homing Pigeon World, telephone 01938 552360 or visit their website www.pigeonracing.com.

An alternative is to release helium balloons. At the ceremony in the picture, everyone stood still, transfixed, as the balloons rose steeply into the blue sky, soon becoming smaller and smaller, signifying the rising up of the spirit.

Often funerals gather together families and friends who have not seen each other for a long time. It was neither the time nor place to swap stories before the funeral, but gathering together afterwards provides a more relaxed atmosphere in which to chat and re-adjust. The process of renewing friendships, remembering, exchanging news and eating helps bring people back to the everyday world. If there is a wide range of age groups, it is often babies and young children who break the ice and help the adults to smile again.

All are not taken; there are left behind
Living beloveds, tender looks to bring
And make the daylight still a happy thing,
And tender voices, to make soft the mind

extract from 'Consolation'
Elizabeth Barrett Browning

95 the gathering after the funeral

Choosing a place to meet can cause a lot of uncertainty. Unlike a wedding, you never know how many people are going to arrive and therefore how big a space you need or how many to cater for. The only realistic thing to do is to make an informed guess at numbers and make your decisions accordingly.

- if you need to keep an eye on your budget and not spend what you cannot afford, you could ask everyone to bring food and drink to share. People often like to do this as it gives them a sense of involvement and nowadays it is not frowned upon as it once might have been
- choose and book in advance an appropriate venue, not too far from where the ceremony was held. If necessary print off a map and send it out in advance
- if you feel you can ask people home, you will definitely need help to prepare the space, cater and clear up afterwards
- often extended family and friends will volunteer to take over the organisation of the gathering. Let them, as long as you are satisfied their endeavours will be appropriate to the occasion
- if you have chosen to make a photo montage take it along or leave family photos out for people to look at. There could be a book where people can write messages, thoughts, memories and wishes
- take into account that those who have long journeys home will not want to leave too late

96 **ceremonial food**

Choosing, preparing and sharing food can be a wonderful part of the gathering after the funeral.

P was buried in a field, dedicated to his memory, on his own smallholding, one day in late spring. A local chef had been asked to prepare a simple hot meal for about sixty people. Long trestle tables had been set up outside one of the barns

and everyone was served a bowl of piping hot stew with a great crust of brown bread, just as P loved to entertain.

After V's funeral at the crematorium, everyone was given instructions as to how to drive to her favourite tea shop on the cliff overlooking the sea. We had to park and then walk along the cliff top for a little while just as V used to. The sea was very blue, the sky clear and the tea shop provided a wonderful selection of hot soup, savoury snacks and cakes on silver cake stands with tea in china cups.

Dia de los Muertos – the Mexican Day of the Dead festival, is when ceremonial food is prepared without equal. From 31st October to 2nd November, Mexicans celebrate the reunion of dead relatives with their families. Colourfully decorated altars are set up at home with flowers, pictures and sumptuous foods to entice the departed souls back home and provide them with food and adequate sustenance for their journey. This varies from spicy sauces with meat and chicken, chocolate beverages and bottles of beer to sugary confections in a variety of animal and skull shapes and special egg-batter breads. It is a festival of reunion and celebration where death is accepted as a part of everyday life, and if you bite into the plastic skeleton the baker placed in the rounded *Pan de Muertos* (Bread of the Dead) you are considered really lucky!

The Mexican Day of the Dead inspired the Natural Death Centre to organise the UK. Day of the Dead, held annually in April. The annual celebration of art, music, poetry, theatre and discussion is co-ordinated with open days at natural burial grounds, with the aim of helping us to commemorate and celebrate our loved ones, and to keep our own sense of death in perspective, by giving death and the dead a time as well as a place.

memorials

Our private and public lives are punctuated with memorial ceremonies throughout the year. Whether we choose to take part in the memorials for the World Wars, or light a candle on an anniversary of the death of a loved one, we are aware of days with special significance and of time passing.

Funerals themselves often pass in a blur of grief and confusion, very soon after death. If the circumstances were such that many people could not attend the funeral, or the family chose to hold it privately, or there is an irreconcilable difference of opinion in a family or between family and friends, there is a second opportunity for everyone to gain a sense of completion, if a memorial ceremony is held. Any time after the funeral, perhaps within a few weeks, perhaps on the first anniversary of the death, can be appropriate. Whatever time interval elapses, you will have more time to think, to plan and gather people together.

A memorial ceremony can take many different forms, either a full ceremony (with or without the ashes present) or a brief, informal, few words when the ashes are scattered or interred, or a tree planted. It could be a dinner or party in honour of the person. Some families meet up, light a candle and have a special meal on each anniversary of the birth, or death, of the person. If a well-known figure has died, a more public memorial often follows a private family funeral, and this is often the chosen format following a controversial death when the family need privacy.

Memorials can be much more private. Each year, many people refer to the ashes in memory. Others find a way to remember someone quietly at home.

97 scattering and interring the ashes

Before interring D's ashes in a woodland burial site, his urn was passed from person to person and each either said something privately or out loud. Some took off the lid so they could see and touch them.

The number of people collecting ashes from the crematoria has more than quadrupled over the last thirty-five years. In order to dispose of these ashes, at least two hundred thousand private ceremonies of some sort are conducted every year in the UK. These largely private, informal, family-led ceremonies offer redemption over the standardised professional procedures at the crematoria.

The good thing about ashes is the ease with which you can scatter or inter them, at a place which has happy memories and which you can visit in the future. Remember to be considerate in terms of where you choose to scatter ashes. The National Parks are expressing concern at the amount of ashes scattered on popular summits. A large volume of ashes has the ability to change the existing delicate ecosystem. The Environment Agency is also considering prohibiting the strewing of ashes in popular stretches of river and their guidelines should be followed.

There do not appear to be any laws or national regulations to stop you scattering or interring ashes, except that you should gain the permission of the owner of the land. If you want to open an existing grave in order to inter ashes, you need permission to do so from the church or cemetery authorities. You should not scatter them in a churchyard, from a harbour wall or pier without permission of the vicar, harbour master or pier master. See page 170.

You do not need a licence to scatter ashes at sea offshore. You could hire a self-drive boat or there are skippered boats that will take you.

Local authorities often give local guidelines about scattering ashes, including

advice on times of day – early in the morning or towards dusk – and to be sensitive to passers by and people who are out and about.

An adult's ashes amount to around a two-litre volume of gritty dust, so be aware of the wind direction! If you want to keep the ashes at home, you can simply keep them in a beautiful urn or lidded jar.

Environment Agency guidelines concerning the spreading of ashes on water.

Do not

- spread ashes within 1 km upstream of any drinking-water supply
- use a bridge over a river used by boaters and canoeists
- use a marina or anywhere close to anglers
- hold ceremonies in very windy weather or close to buildings. Spread the ashes as close to the surface of the water as possible
- allow other objects containing metal and plastic to enter the water
- use busy spots or where the water is obviously used for commercial, agricultural, or recreational purposes or for drinking

98 **turn the ashes into an object**

For an unusual, permanent and dazzling memento, you can have the ashes turned into a gem stone like a diamond. Or you can have some of the ashes incorporated into a glass vase or paper weight. The vase in the picture was made by the Winnie Glass Company (see page 192).

You can also mix them with clay or concrete to make something that includes the ashes in its fabric. In Buddhist tradition, a figure of a Buddha is made by combining the ashes of a devotee with clay.

The flame of your brave soul shot such heat and light
as burnt our earth and made our darkness bright.

adapted from Thomas Carew (1595–1639)

Memorial Ceremony for Mum – John's Story

Mum died one year after my dad, who was buried in the family grave with my two grandmothers. Just across the way is my brother Antony's grave. Her wish was to be cremated as there was no room for her in either grave and she wanted her ashes to be put on both graves.

At the time of the first anniversary of her death, I wrote to all the important close family and friends announcing the date for the interment of her ashes and offering the opportunity for anyone who desired to contribute memories or poems associated with Mum. I wanted it to be a shared experience as much as possible. I had also had a new headstone made to include Dad and Mum.

There were about twenty-five family members at the graveside, on a very cold Sunday afternoon in February. I had visited the graves the day before and prepared the ground for the ceremony by removing a square foot of turf on both graves under which we would spread her ashes.

I welcomed the gathering, outlined the proceedings and relayed Mum's wishes for her ashes to be put on the graves of her loved ones. Mum always believed that in death she would be reunited with her family who had passed away. My brother had been tragically killed in a motorcycle accident at sixteen and we were now symbolically performing the ritual of that reunification. We had all shared in that impossible suffering since 'the accident' and felt the poignancy and the relief now that the grief could be put to rest. Mum had carried the tragedy all her life.

After my introduction, my daughter read a poem by Mary Oliver called 'White Owl Flies Into and Out of the Field' and her sister read one about a ship sailing away over the horizon. I peeled back the turfs on both the graves and passed round the pottery jar containing Mum's ashes, inviting each person to take a handful for each grave. We all planted a pansy in a hole, to make the shape of a heart around where we had put the ashes. My hope is that each year the pansies will flower at the time of their anniversary.

I closed the ceremony and we left the cemetery for a local restaurant, where we chatted for a couple of hours before the long journeys home.

Everybody said how they appreciated taking part, they all felt personally involved in the ceremony, saying their heartfelt goodbye to Mum.

99 the content of a memorial service

The form and content of a memorial service usually focuses more on the life, contributions and memories of the person and less on the loss. If many of those gathered missed the funeral, it is more important to mark the loss, perhaps symbolically through the lighting and extinguishing of a candle.

The memorial may seek to remind everyone of the ongoing nature of the spirit of the person, at least in memory. The love for the person remains, and the feelings evoked through stories and memories can be as vivid as when first experienced, but with an added poignancy.

Many of the ideas discussed in the ceremonies section apply to a memorial service, such as if it is to be run by the family or a conductor/celebrant, religious or secular, where it takes place, decoration, words and music.

A person lives for as long as she is carried in the hearts of others.
What the heart has once known it will never forget.

Anon

100 **a private place for contemplation**

The loss of someone close can be unbearable, and there is often a need to maintain a feeling of closeness before being able to let go completely. By setting aside a space within a room, it is possible to create a memorial place at home. Decorate it with pictures, flowers, candles, treasured objects, a walking stick, letters and it can become a place to sit quietly and remember. Also, it can prompt visitors to talk more openly about the person who has died, which is often the conversation most needed by those left behind. Over time, the place will change until all that is needed may be a photo.

A garden is perfect for dedicating a space for quiet contemplation. How far you develop this is entirely your choice, perhaps a simple statue or an engraving will be suitable but as the seasons and the flowers and foliage change, so will the feelings of grief.

101 **a woodland dedication**

Sometimes it is difficult to know where to place a donation of money, especially if the person died unexpectedly leaving no directives or clues. The well-known and well-established charities for cancer research or hospice care are popular choices. Another possibility is to create a woodland memorial site. This type of memorial is not only beautiful, but also has long-term environmental benefits. Because nearly half of Britain's ancient woodland has been lost in the last seventy years, by choosing to dedicate woodland as a tribute to a loved one you will help to prevent the loss of more ancient woodland, and to contribute new native woods for future generations to enjoy.

If you are interested in finding out more about this, The Woodland Trust (see page 194) cares for more than a thousand woods throughout the UK and it is possible for you to choose to dedicate a piece of woodland which will be near somewhere special to you. Via this organisation, each woodland area is dedicated only once, linking a life exclusively and for ever with a piece of beautiful natural landscape; anywhere from Cornwall to the Scottish Highlands.

resources
and information